THE CIVIL SERVICE
IN BRITAIN AND FRANCE

Works by
Professor William A. Robson

★

GREAT CITIES OF THE WORLD: THEIR GOVERNMENT,
POLITICS AND PLANNING
PROBLEMS OF NATIONALIZED INDUSTRY
THE RELATION OF WEALTH TO WELFARE
THE LAW OF LOCAL GOVERNMENT AUDIT
JUSTICE AND ADMINISTRATIVE LAW
CIVILIZATION AND THE GROWTH OF LAW
THE GOVERNMENT AND MISGOVERNMENT OF LONDON
THE DEVELOPMENT OF LOCAL GOVERNMENT
THE BRITISH SYSTEM OF GOVERNMENT
THE UNIVERSITY TEACHING OF POLITICAL SCIENCE
THE TOWN COUNCILLOR (WITH C. R. ATTLEE)

Contributor to
BRITISH GOVERNMENT SINCE 1918

Edited by William A. Robson
THE BRITISH CIVIL SERVANT
PUBLIC ENTERPRISE
SOCIAL SECURITY

Joint Editor with H. J. Laski and W. I. Jennings
A CENTURY OF MUNICIPAL PROGRESS

THE CIVIL SERVICE

IN BRITAIN AND FRANCE

Edited by
WILLIAM A. ROBSON

*Professor of Public Administration
at the London School of Economics
and Political Science (University
of London)*

1956
THE HOGARTH PRESS
LONDON

PUBLISHED BY
THE HOGARTH PRESS LTD
LONDON

★

CLARKE IRWIN AND CO LTD
TORONTO

PRINTED IN GREAT BRITAIN BY
ROBERT CUNNINGHAM AND SONS LTD., ALVA

CONTENTS

v

FOREWORD

NINE of the essays in this book originally appeared in a
special number of *The Political Quarterly* for October-
December 1954. The special number was devoted to the Civil
Service to mark the centenary of the Trevelyan-Northcote reforms of 1854. But its purpose was not only to look backwards
along the path we have travelled during the past century but
to consider the Civil Service in relation to its present tasks and
the emerging needs of the British people.

The special number of the review was quickly sold out, and
the demand from home and overseas readers was so great that
a second printing was required.

In view of the continuing interest of students, officials, political scientists, sociologists, politicians, journalists and citizens
in the Civil Service and its problems, it was decided to publish
the essays in a more permanent form. They embody an exceptional range of knowledge and experience of Ministerial office,
the highest positions in the Civil Service, and University teaching and research.

The authors have in most instances revised or expanded their
original essays. This applies to chapters 3, 4, 5, 6, 8, 9 and 12. In
addition, five entirely new essays have been specially written
for the book and are now published for the first time. These
are: Bureaucracy and Democracy by William A. Robson; The
Colonial Service by The Right Hon. A. Creech Jones, M.P.; Civil
Service Establishments and the Treasury by Sir Thomas Padmore; Whitley Councils in the Civil Service by Douglas Hough-
ton, M.P.; and the Recruitment and Training of Higher Civil
Servants in the United Kingdom and in France by André
Bertrand.

I should like to express my gratitude to those who have co-
operated so generously in this literary enterprise, sometimes
in ways which are not visible. My thanks are also due to Miss
Jennifer Hines, who compiled the index, read the final proofs,
and assisted me in other ways.

W. A. R.

Chapter 1

BUREAUCRACY AND DEMOCRACY

By WILLIAM A. ROBSON

THERE is much talk in the press and on the platform about bureaucracy. The subject is one of immense importance, and it is desirable that it should be widely discussed, though with more insight and understanding than is commonly shown.

What do we mean by bureaucracy? Max Weber, whose writings originated the modern study of bureaucracy, identified it with the following characteristics: first, the allocation as official duties of the regular activities needed to fulfil the purposes of the organ; second, the distribution in a stable manner of the authority required to discharge these duties, and its strict delimitation by rules concerning the means of enforcement available to officials; third, methodical provision for the regular performance of these functions by qualified persons. Weber regarded these three elements as constituting 'bureaucratic authority' in public administration, or 'bureaucratic management' in private enterprise. He further observed in all bureaucratic structures the hierarchical principle; a reliance on written documents, files, records, and the apparatus of modern office management; the formulation of general rules or practices for the management of the office, these rules comprising a technique in which the officials of both public and private administration must be trained, and in which they become expert.[1]

Professor Friedrich of Harvard has carried the analysis a stage further and suggests six primary criteria of bureaucracy. These are differentiation of functions; qualifications for office; hierarchical organization and discipline; objectivity of method; precision and consistency or continuity, involving adherence to rules, 'red tape' and the keeping of records; and lastly, the exercise of discretion, involving secrecy in regard to certain aspects of government.[2]

[1] Max Weber: *Essays in Sociology* (Ed. Gerth & Mills), pp. 197-198.
[2] *Constitutional Government and Democracy* (2nd Edition, 1951), pp. 57-58.

1

Many other American political scientists have written on bureaucracy but their definitions do not always agree. Professor Herbert A. Simon regards it as an approximate synonym for large-scale organization[1]; Dean Paul Appleby says that it is inseparable from 'the phenomenon of systematic interaction of many persons associated in common and complex terms'.[2]

It is obvious that bureaucracy is not confined to government but exists in a wide variety of institutions, such as banks, insurance companies, railways, commercial and industrial concerns, professional associations, trade unions and trade associations, churches, political parties, voluntary societies, hospitals and universities. Professor Wheare has pointed out that there are far more bureaucrats outside government service than within it. Moreover, he rightly insists that the state must have its own bureaucracy if it is to hold its own with or control other institutions possessing their own powerful bureaucracies.[3] Most people wrongly assume that bureaucracy is found only in public authorities; but we need not pursue this point since here we are concerned entirely with the sphere of government.

Bureaucracy is clearly indispensable to modern government. This is not merely because it is far more efficient than the older methods of working and of management which it has superseded, but also because it is a levelling, rationalizing force. It uses objective methods of recruitment in place of nepotism and patronage; it seeks to promote according to merit rather than for political or personal reasons. It administers on the basis of rules, precedents and policy rather than on grounds of personal feelings, influence or favouritism. It tries to formulate quantitative measurements of efficiency. It aims at consistency of treatment in its dealings with the public. These and many other advantages are derived from modern bureaucratic administration.

The man in the street, the journalist, and most politicians persist in regarding bureaucracy as synonymous with the maladies from which it sometimes suffers. That it does suffer from maladies on occasion is uncontestable, but it is wrong to identify bureaucracy with its failings and to condemn it out of hand on

---

[1] Herbert A. Simon: 'Staff and Management Controls' in *The Annals of the American Academy of Political and Social Science* (March 1954), p. 95.
[2] Paul H. Appleby: 'Bureaucracy and the Future' *ibid.* p. 138.
[3] K. C. Wheare: *The Machinery of Government* (Oxford, 1945), pp. 7-9.

account of them. Whatever else may happen, bureaucracy has come to stay. We should be wise to accept it as a necessary element in the modern world and do our utmost to improve it. We should be fully alive to the dangers which threaten both the individual citizen and the community when bureaucracy becomes diseased.

The tone and temper of much of the literature of protest which has appeared in recent decades are not likely to add to our understanding of the problems associated with bureaucracy or to our solving them. Books like Lord Hewart's *New Despotism*, James Beck's *Our Wonderland of Bureaucracy*, Sir Carleton Allen's *Bureaucracy Triumphant* and his more recent *Law and Orders* are well-known examples of this literature and there are many others. Books of this kind—and the same is true of the newspapers—generally use the word bureaucracy as a term of invective, representing what an American writer calls 'the language of contempt'.[1] Some of the recent writing in the United States is far more serious and penetrating than anything which has appeared in this country.[2]

The maladies from which bureaucracy most frequently suffers are an excessive sense of self-importance on the part of officials or an undue idea of the importance of their office; an indifference towards the feelings or the convenience of individual citizens; an obsession with the binding and inflexible authority of departmental decisions, precedents, arrangements or forms, regardless of how badly or with what injustice they may work in individual cases; a mania for regulations and formal procedure; a preoccupation with the activities of particular units of administration and an inability to consider the government as a whole; a failure to recognize the relations between the governors and

[1] 'Bureaucracy—Fact and Fiction' by John A. Vieg in *Elements of Public Administration* edited by M. Morstein Marx (New York, 1946), p. 5. See also the Report of IPSA conference on Comparative Public Administration with special reference to Bureaucracy, p.3.

[2] See, for example, Paul H. Appleby: *Big Democracy* (New York, 1945); 'Bureaucracy and Democratic Government' in *The Annals of the American Academy of Political and Social Science* (March 1954); A. W. Gouldner: *Studies in Leadership* (New York, 1950); R. K. Merton, A. P. Gray, B. Hockey and H. A. Selvin (Editors) *Reader in Bureaucracy* (Glencoe, Ill., 1952); Morstein Marx: *Elements of Public Administration* (New York, 1946); Charles S. Hyneman: *Bureaucracy in a Democracy* (New York, 1950).

the governed as an essential part of the democratic process.

The most hopeful way of avoiding or curing these deficiencies does not lie in reviving ancient battle cries derived from constitutional struggles in past centuries or in yielding to facile denunciation and righteous indignation. We must seek rather to discover the methods by which administration can be made or kept democratic, or more consistent with democracy, and this involves a positive approach.

In his excellent book *Bureaucracy in a Democracy*,[1] Professor Charles S. Hyneman begins by stating four assumptions. First, the conviction that bureaucracy must be judged by the way it uses its power, and not by its size and cost. Second, that all those who possess governmental authority should exercise their power within limits that are acceptable to the nation as a whole. Third, the belief that the powers which modern bureaucracy possesses can be turned towards ends that are not acceptable to the people as a whole, and may be turned towards them if proper direction and control over administration are not provided. Fourth, that we must chiefly rely on elective officials— or as we should say, Ministers and politicians—to carry out the task of control and direction. Professor Hyneman points out that by far the most important factor in determining the size and cost of the civil service is the scope of governmental activity. The need for critical analysis of our administrative arrangements arises from the question of whether and how we can direct and control bureaucracy, irrespective of its size.[2]

These assumptions are sound in principle, and apply with equal validity to the situation in Great Britain and other countries no less than in the United States. Too much emphasis has been placed on mere bigness as a formative element in producing bureaucracy. Hyneman himself falls into the error of saying that bureaucracy as an abstraction is big organization, and any big organization is, specifically, a bureaucracy.[3] American political scientists very often identify bigness with bureaucracy. Professor Wheare, on the other hand, regards solicitors as the archbureaucrats because they cannot give a straightforward answer to a simple question.[4] I have myself observed bureaucracies in

---

[1] Harper & Bros. (New York, 1950), pp. 5-6. [2] *Ib.* p. 10.
[3] *Ib.* p. 3. See also, Paul H. Appleby: *Big Democracy* (New York, 1945) Ch. II. [4] K. C. Wheare: *op. cit.* p. 7.

small countries, and in some of them I have seen many of the bureaucratic maladies in an advanced state.

In much of what has been written on this point the authors omit to state whether the 'bigness' which results in bureaucracy is the large size of the country concerned; or the existence of very large units of administration, such as Ministries or Departments; or the total numbers employed in the civil service, considered either absolutely or as a percentage of the population. Each of these criteria of bigness would yield different results.

The identification of bigness with bureaucracy has led politicians and publicists who are hostile to the expanded functions of the modern state to allege that if the activities of government are as wide as they are today in most countries, morbid bureaucracy is inevitable; and the only way of curing or avoiding it is to curtail the scope of governmental action. Hence, much of the opposition to and denunciation of bureaucracy springs from the reactionary politics of those who are in substance opposing the welfare policies of the modern state. Nothing fruitful is likely to emerge from an attitude which postulates that the best method of solving the problems of public administration in the welfare state is to put the clock back a hundred years and return to the halcyon days when the executive did almost nothing judged by modern standards.

Some interesting propositions were advanced at a conference on comparative public administration held in Paris by the International Political Science Association in 1953. During a session devoted to 'Recent developments in the theory of Democratic Administration',[1] Monsieur Pujet, a councillor of the *Conseil d'État*, argued that in order to be considered democratic an administration must satisfy three criteria: First, it must be open in the sense of having wide contacts with the people. It must not operate in the interest of the ruler or of a directing class. It must be recruited without discrimination from a very broad social strata. It must maintain contact with the public through consultation, inquiries and procedures which enable it to be aware of the state of mind of the governed. It must avoid an arrogant disposition.

[1] Report of a Conference held by the International Political Science Association on Comparative Public Administration with special reference to Bureaucracy: published by IPSA, p. 17.

Second, the administration must be controlled not only by an official hierarchy or the jurisdictional power (that is, the right of review given to the administrative tribunals) but also by public opinion and public liberties, such as the freedom of the press, the right of association, and the right of demonstration. The people and their representatives must be free to discuss and to criticize the administration.

Third, administrative power must be subordinate and submissive. Administrative power should not exist independently of political power. On the other hand, civil servants must not be completely subordinate and the administration must be independent of interference by political parties. A political party in power should not try to monopolize all the jobs or to exercise pressure on responsible civil servants. The principle of continuity of administration must be maintained. Ministers are of course entitled to exercise authority over civil servants; what is deprecated is any form of direct pressure by a political party on public officials.

Professor R. Aron, the French sociologist and writer, insisted that the essential criteria of democracy in administration include decentralization; the subordination of administration to policies which reflect the desires of the people; and a friendly attitude on the part of officials towards the governed.

These remarks by MM. Pujet and Aron would command a substantial measure of agreement in Britain, the Commonwealth, the United States, and elsewhere. The stress laid on the avoidance of arrogance and the cultivation of a friendly attitude towards the public are exactly the qualities which the ordinary Englishman regards as outward signs that administration is democratic in spirit. It is the presence of such qualities which bridges the gulf between 'we' and 'they' that often separates the governors from the governed. The existence of such a gulf is opposed both to the interests of good administration and of democracy.

We may turn from these general reflections to consider the rôle of the Civil Service in a parliamentary democracy, with particular reference to the British system.

It will be agreed that the honour of the British Civil Service has reached a very high level. The defection of Burgess and Maclean is the first serious instance of corruption involving civil servants since the Francs case of 1928. The Civil Service came out of the unpleasant affairs investigated by the Lynskey Tribunal with quite clean hands. This bright record has been maintained despite the fact that in recent decades, and especially between 1939 and 1950, the opportunities for corruption must have increased vastly owing to state trading on a gigantic scale, rationing, requisitioning, the bulk buying of foodstuffs and raw materials, and the receipt of lend-lease supplies. This is enormously to the credit of the Service.

In the second place we have managed to keep our Civil Service under effective political control by Ministers and the Cabinet. This does not by any means automatically occur in a parliamentary system. It requires a powerful political government which depends in turn on the constitution, on the party system, on the relations between Parliament and the Executive, and on the relations between Ministers and civil servants. In Sweden, for example, only a very small proportion of the Civil Service is under the day-to-day control of Ministers. The great bulk of the central services are administered by boards of civil servants who are about as free from detailed ministerial control as our nationalized industries. One important fact which is usually overlooked is that in this country political reform preceded civil service reform, so that a reformed House of Commons and a government supported by it were in a strong position relatively to the Civil Service. Germany, on the other hand, established very efficient and strong bureaucracies long before political reforms of a democratic character were introduced; and this made it difficult for Ministers and the elective element to gain effective control over officials.

There are, in the Cabinet system of government, three principal factors in the parliamentary equation: Ministers, Members of Parliament, and civil servants. They comprise the essential elements, representative or bureaucratic; and they are indispensable to one another. They are partners in a common enterprise—'the endless adventure of governing men'. Unless the terms of the partnership are understood and accepted by all the partners the enterprise may not succeed. Yet surprisingly little has been written on the relations between Ministers and officials. Some interesting remarks were, however, made by Mr Herbert Morrison and the then Home Secretary, Sir David Maxwell

Fyfe (now Lord Kilmuir), during the House of Commons debate on Critchel Down.[1] Mr Herbert Morrison expressed the view that a Minister need not always defend his officials in public, and he mentioned that on one occasion he had, as a Minister, publicly castigated in Parliament an official of his department who had failed to carry out his instructions. Usually, however, the Minister accepts responsibility for the acts of his officials even when he does not approve of them. Sir David Maxwell Fyfe, speaking as Home Secretary, agreed broadly with Mr Morrison's view that a Minister is under no obligation to endorse what he believes to be wrong or to defend the manifest errors of his officers. He need not approve of action which he knew nothing about and of which he disapproves; but he will nevertheless remain constitutionally responsible to Parliament for the fact that something has gone wrong, and can be called to account for it.

In theory, Ministers decide policy, and civil servants carry out their decisions. This is strictly true from a constitutional standpoint; but in reality it is a conventional half-truth. Ministers seldom have the time, or knowledge, and sometimes not the skill, to formulate policy unaided. They must rely on their senior officials for advice, and still more for knowledge of the basic facts and figures on which policy must be based. They have a right to expect that civil servants will do their utmost to make proposals which will reflect, or at least be compatible with, the political philosophy and the programme of the party in power.

A Minister should always consult his senior officials before deciding an important matter of policy, though he is not under a legal or constitutional duty to do so. One compelling consideration is that if he blunders, the department, as well as he personally, will suffer a loss of reputation. The civil servant on his side has a right to put forward what Sir Edward Bridges has called 'the Departmental philosophy'. It is, indeed, his duty to give his Minister the quintessence of departmental experience on those large issues of policy which he must decide and thus 'to let the waves of the practical philosophy wash against ideas put forward by his Ministerial master'.[2] The civil servant is

---

[1] Parliamentary Debates. H.o.C. 20th July 1954, Vol. 530, Cols. 1274-94.
[2] *Portrait of a Profession*, p. 19.

entitled to advise, to warn, to encourage and to explain—but no more. Sir Ernest Gowers has gone so far as to say that if a civil servant thinks a proposal by his Minister is misconceived, it is his duty to say so, and why. He may, if invited to do so, express his opinion as to the relative advantages and disadvantages of alternative courses of action, looked at from the government's standpoint. He must not, however, allow his personal prejudices or his political bias to suppress or distort policies or to denigrate courses of action which are administratively practicable although leading to ends he considers to be undesirable. If he feels very strongly opposed to a course of action which the government has decided upon, he should ask for a transfer to another department. This will rarely occur.

Above all, a civil servant has no right to be unhelpful, unconstructive, and negative. Nor should he be indifferent to the political convictions or party pressures which affect the Minister he serves. Although as an official he may not share them, he should nonetheless be aware of their existence and make due allowances for them in his work. Civil servants will, however, be acting without the knowledge or guidance of their political chiefs most of the time; and hence it is important that they should accurately reflect the Minister's mind or at least his policy in every aspect of day-to-day administration. This should apply right down the line, subject to the important qualification that the vast majority of departmental decisions are non-political.

If departmental administration is accurately to reflect the Minister's outlook, civil servants of all ranks—and not only one or two at the top of the departmental pyramid—must be brought into contact with the Minister and thereby learn his views. This is particularly important when there is a change of government, or when one Minister succeeds another. Talks by the Minister to staff gatherings, and other methods of achieving personal contact, can bring great advantages which will well repay the time and trouble spent on them. The wider the range of officials who can have occasional, or even frequent access to the Minister the better for all concerned. Mutual understanding, respect and confidence between a Minister and his officials should be based on a firm foundation of knowledge; and time occupied in ensuring this is well spent. Higher officials should in their turn make continuous efforts to see that everyone below them understands the Minister's policy. Various devices can be used for this purpose, such as staff meetings, house organs, explanatory talks by the most senior officials, and so forth. There is much scope for an expansion of internal information services within departments.

These remarks about the relations between Ministers and officials may sound platitudinous, but the propositions they contain by no means reflect the everyday practices of all departments. The political control of the civil service is not only essential to administration in a democracy, but involves so much more than the simple statement that the civil service is subordinate to Ministers, that I make no excuse for pursuing the matter a little further.

There is a sound rule which requires Members of Parliament to communicate with the Minister in charge of a department and not to make a direct approach to his officials, except with his knowledge and permission. The dangers of a too close relationship between Members of Parliament and civil servants might be considerable. A civil servant might be deflected by the political influence of an M.P. or a group of M.P.s. He might be made to feel that his own future depended to some extent on the favour or disfavour in which he stood with members of the legislature—a frequent phenomenon in the U.S., where the relations between the civil service and the Congress are much closer than they are here. A Minister's authority in his department might be undermined by legislative support for a particular division or branch. Above all, the status of Ministers in Parliament would be lowered if M.P.s could get what they wanted by going behind their backs to officials.

In a paper presented to the conference mentioned above, Mr Aron remarked that it is doubtful whether even the most highly placed bureaucrats can aspire to a leading rôle in modern society. The leaders of modern societies, he declared, direct bureaucracies and they need bureaucracies; but does it follow they are representatives of bureaucracies? Their power may come from another source.[1] The answer to such a question must obviously depend on the relative positions of the political and the administrative elements. In France, for example, the position of Ministers is exceptionally weak owing to the intransigence, hostility

[1] *Report (op. cit.)* p. 2.

and irresponsibility of the legislature towards the political executive. An indirect consequence of this is to strengthen the position of the Civil Service, although any tendency towards arbitrary administrative action is restrained by the excellent system of judicial review provided by the *Conseil d'État*.[1] In Britain, leadership does not rest with the Civil Service, although it plays a vitally important part in carrying on the work of government.

We may turn from these general considerations concerning the relation of politics to administration to the question of the location of power and the organization of authority. I am convinced that excessive centralization tends to produce some of the commonest diseases of bureaucracy: remoteness, inflexibility, insensitiveness, ignorance of local conditions, procrastination, clumsiness and complacency. I therefore agree with Professor Aron that a substantial measure of decentralization is necessary to bring administration into line with democratic ideas. This will necessitate not only the devolution of power to elected authorities at the local and regional levels; but also the deconcentration of power from central Ministries to civil servants in the field. I am well aware of the problems involved in allocating discretionary powers throughout a large department with many local offices; but they can and must be solved.

Every modern nation needs a strong executive possessing adequate power to enable it to carry out the immense tasks which governments are expected to fulfil today. But the very fact of this unquestionable need makes it all the more important that the executive should not be uncontrolled. We have already considered political control and I am thinking now of judicial control. The administrative process is largely concerned nowadays with social services, economic or military questions, which will affect thousands or millions of persons. In the course of administration a department can by sheer inadvertence quite easily ride roughshod over the interests of an individual citizen. Sometimes, as in the case of Critchel Down, the arbitrary or harsh treatment of an individual is not due to inadvertence. Whatever the cause may be, an aggrieved citizen should always have an opportunity to lay his complaint before an administrative

[1] For a good recent account see C. J. Hamson: *Executive Discretion and Judicial Control. passim.*

tribunal possessing sufficient power and knowledge to probe the matter thoroughly and provide an adequate remedy. Unless judicial review in this comprehensive sense is readily available to the citizen of small means I do not see how a system of administration can be called fully democratic or subject to the rule of law. We do not have such opportunities for judicial review in Britain today. The legal profession and the political parties are at last becoming uncomfortably aware of the serious consequences of our prolonged refusal to grapple with the problem of providing the individual with a legal safeguard against possible injustice at the hands of the administrative state. The old *clichés* about the rule of law have died away. Whether we shall be willing to innovate with sufficient boldness and understanding to meet the need is by no means certain.

The Civil Service is far from indifferent to public opinion of certain kinds. It is exceedingly sensitive to parliamentary opinion, especially that of the House of Commons. It is also highly sensitive to the views of large and powerful organizations, such as the T.U.C., the National Union of Farmers, the National Union of Teachers, or the British Medical Association. But the Service is much less sensitive to the views or feelings of ordinary citizens, partly because they are usually unorganized, and partly because, except during elections, they have less influence with Ministers. One of the weak spots of some civil servants is the tendency to regard as unimportant an incident which may have created violent indignation among a few families in a village. We—or is it they?—have become too statistical in our perception of what is important.

Today we live in a pluralist society, whatever the theory of government may be. Organized groups representing vocational, professional, religious, and social interests dominate the scene; and these groups are consulted by government departments at many different stages in the formulation of policy, the preparation of legislation, and the conduct of administration. This pluralism is not objectionable in principle, and in practice it has many advantages. A governmental programme, it has been well said, does not exist for its own sake, but as a part of a larger purpose related to the social order.[1] These great group associ-

---

[1] Don Price: 'Democratic Administration' in *Elements of Public Administration* edited by Morstein Marx. *op. cit.* p. 81.

ations, which are pressing on government all the time in one way or another, are very much part of the social order. It is easy to concede that government should co-operate with them. The problem is 'to keep the system of co-operative government from freezing into a structure of guilds or competing pressure groups.'[1]

The Civil Service comes into frequent contact with the groups which exist; it feels their influence and hears their highly articulate demands. But what about the interests which are not organized and not articulate? There is a highly vocal old persons lobby, the British Legion represents the ex-service men, and innumerable trade unions, professional and trade associations defend and advance powerful vocational or sectional interests. Concessions are made all the time to these bodies. But children are not organized; nor are housewives; nor are widows; nor are deaf persons; nor schedule E taxpayers. Where there is no pressure from an organized group, civil servants may too easily assume that all is well and nothing need be done. It is a poor conception of democratic administration which considers that the benefits of government shall go mainly to the most powerful and vociferous groups. Neither civil servants or Ministers would accept such a bald proposition; but something very like it can easily come about in practice unless both civil servants and Ministers possess considerable imagination and have a wide-ranging view of society. Witness, for example, the unjustifiably favourable position accorded to the medical profession as a result of the efforts of the British Medical Association.

It follows from what has been said that the Civil Service must be completely integrated in the community if the spirit of democracy is to permeate the administrative process. We have already made considerable advances in that direction in recent decades; further movement can and should be made. Civil servants are themselves anxious to break down the restrictions and conventions which in the past tended to set them apart as a separate caste or class. The policy of the Treasury in giving facilities to enable civil servants to accept Commonwealth Fellowships, temporary fellowships at Nuffield College and the London School of Economics and Political Science, to attend courses at the

---

[1] Don Price: 'Democratic Administration' in *Elements of Public Administration* edited by Morstein Marx. *op. cit.* p. 87.

Administrative Staff College, and so forth, has been helpful. But this is only a beginning and it would be a great exaggeration to say that the gulf between 'we' and 'they' has been wholly bridged.

One aspect of integration is that the Civil Service should be broadly representative of the various social and economic classes in the community. In the past, the higher Civil Service has been drawn predominantly from a privileged minority, as Mr Kelsall's investigations show. This is less marked today, but the chances of a higher civil servant having come from a working-class home are still very small. We should undoubtedly place the chief emphasis on administrative ability and high intellectual capacity in recruiting the Administrative Class and promoting men to the higher positions; but a strong effort must be made to see that this vital part of the Service, and also the Foreign Service, is not too much dominated by those coming from one favoured group.

A second objective should be to attain an effective and continuous system of communication between the governors and the governed: which in this context means between government departments and those sections of the public which they serve or control. I have referred elsewhere in this book[1] to the various methods and devices which have been introduced for this purpose and I shall therefore do no more than mention them as an indispensable instrument for bringing government and citizens to a closer mutual understanding and thereby promoting democratic administration. It is worth noticing that the malevolent attacks on the public relations and information services of government departments has usually come from those who are opposed to the scope and policies of modern government, and are therefore anxious to hamper an improvement in its techniques.[2]

The third objective at which we should aim is widespread participation in the administrative process by persons who are neither professional politicians nor civil servants. We may call this the 'lay' element, though it often possesses high expert

[1] See chapter 5.

[2] American experience is similar to our own in this respect. See Don Price 'Democratic Administration' p. 80 in *Elements of Public Administration* edited by Morstein Marx.

qualifications and experience in particular fields. We already make use of the non-official element to a considerable extent in advisory committees attached to many government departments, such as the Ministry of Education, Ministry of Health, Ministry of Labour and National Service, and the Ministry of National Insurance, which has not only the National Insurance Advisory Committee but several hundred local advisory committees throughout the country. Further developments in this direction are desirable.

In conclusion I would say that integration, communication, and participation should be the watchwords of those who desire to bring public administration into organic relation with the aspirations and needs of democratic government. They indicate the trends of development which, if pursued, will make the Civil Service in the highest degree competent, responsive, and responsible.

Chapter 2

CIVIL SERVANTS, MINISTERS, PARLIAMENT AND THE PUBLIC

By The RIGHT HON. The EARL ATTLEE, O.M.

WHEN I succeeded Mr Churchill as Prime Minister and returned to the conference at Potsdam, I took with me precisely the same team of civil servants, including even the principal private secretary, as had served my predecessor. This occasioned a lively surprise among our American friends who were accustomed to the American system whereby the leading official advisers of the President and of the members of his Cabinet are usually politically of his and their own colour. The incident brought out forcibly the very special position of the British Civil Service, a position which has developed during the past hundred years as the result of the Trevelyan-Northcote reforms.

I do not think that this remarkable attribute of impartiality in the British Civil Service is sufficiently widely known nor adequately recognized for what it is—one of the strongest bulwarks of democracy. I am often at pains to point this out and did so at a conference of Asiatic socialists in Rangoon in 1953 where I told them, to their surprise, that the same men who had worked out the details of Labour's Transport Act were now, at the behest of a Conservative Government, engaged in pulling it to pieces.

I doubt if this impartiality is sufficiently realized even here at home. There were certainly some people in the Labour Party who doubted whether the civil servants would give fair play to a socialist government, but all doubts disappeared with experience.

In this article I propose to say something of the relationship between the civil servant, the Minister, Parliament, and the public, drawing on what has now become a considerable experience.

The first thing a Minister finds on entering office is that he can depend absolutely on the loyalty of his staff and, on leaving office, he will seldom be able to say what the private political views are even of those with whom he has worked most closely. The second thing that he will discover is that the civil servant is prepared to put up every possible objection to his policy, not from a desire to thwart him, but because it is his duty to see that the Minister understands all the difficulties and dangers of the course which he wishes to adopt. Of course, a weak Minister may give way to this opinion voiced by one so much more experienced than himself. This may be gratifying to the civil servant who likes to run the office himself, regarding the Minister as a necessary evil, but, more usually, the Minister who takes this line of least resistance will have forfeited the respect of his staff and, if the Prime Minister is doing his job, will forfeit his office. The strong Minister, on the other hand, will argue with his advisers, refuting, if he can, their arguments and seeking to persuade them of the validity of his point of view. After a reasonable period of discussion, he will say: 'Well, this is my policy, I don't want to argue it any more. Now let us consider how best to implement it.' He will then find the civil servant doing his utmost to help and throwing himself into the work with enthusiasm.

I recall, in this regard, a time when I was working with the late Lord Addison, Minister of Agriculture in the second Labour Government, when he was framing the Agricultural Marketing Bill. Sir Arthur Street, an outstanding civil servant, offered a most strenuous opposition to it, but three weeks later one could have got an affiliation order against him as its only begetter.

Civil servants must develop philosophical minds in relation to Ministers. They have to take what is given to them but, in my opinion, they prefer a 'difficult' Minister to one who is of no account. They like to have someone who will put up a fight, someone in whom they can have some pride.

The civil servant in the higher ranks has not only a long personal experience, but also has that mysterious tradition of the office wherein is somehow embalmed the wisdom of past generations. Of course, sometimes it is necessary to react violently against the tradition which was formed for a different state of society.

I suppose that a good departmental Minister is born not made.

17

There are people who somehow manage to weld the whole of the department into a devoted team. Two men, in my experience, had this gift of inspiring their officials; from the highest to the lowest, in an exceptional degree—Lord Addison and Ernest Bevin.

Lord Addison—or Dr Addison as he then was—managed to get through the House of Commons, although Labour was in a minority, several important Bills. I recall, in particular, the Agricultural Marketing Bill. I remember how he called together the whole of the marketing staff and discussed his proposals with them. Even the most junior was encouraged to make suggestions. In consequence, he got the whole of the department enthusiastically behind him. He had the gift of persuasion which he carried also to the House of Commons where he got not only his own supporters on the committee but eventually his political opponents working as members of a team trying simply to do a good job of work.

It is well known how Ernest Bevin, a man of a very different background from most of the men of the Foreign Service, got not only the respect but the affection of all his staff—from ambassadors to messengers. This was partly due to the fact that he took such pains to see that everyone had a square deal. Every official felt that Ernest Bevin had an interest in him.

The good civil servant studies his Minister's ways and saves him trouble. Some Ministers like to read everything for themselves; others have but a slight appetite for the written word and like what they do read to be predigested. Some like to do their work by personal contact; others are better as correspondents. Some do not know how to concentrate on essentials; others are caught out by lack of attention to detail.

A particular relationship is that between the Minister and his official private secretary. The latter is generally comparatively junior. Appointment to the private office usually means that he is regarded as promising. I always compare this to the appointment of a regimental officer to the staff. Certainly a young man chosen for the Prime Minister's secretariat may congratulate himself on having taken a step up. I have had many private secretaries—all of them very good—yet the post is exacting.

The secretary needs great tact, firstly, in dealing with the Minister and, secondly, in relation to the senior civil servants with whom he is brought into contact. The secretary must study the idiosyncracies of his master and learn how tactfully to prevent him making a blunder. He must know how to help him for Ministers differ very much in their methods of work. He is, too, brought into contact with the Minister's home and family. Here again tact may be required.

I should think that it must be very difficult to switch suddenly after a change of government from serving an adherent of one party to being the helper of a member of another, but I have known private secretaries who have made the transition without apparent difficulty and who have served blue and red with equal loyalty.

The relationship of the high-up civil servant and the junior Minister is sometimes difficult. In the absence of the Minister, the Permanent Secretary considers himself in charge—as indeed he is—but the Under-Secretary is a member of the government and, in particular, is a politician and a member of Parliament. Although new to office and perhaps somewhat raw, he is better versed in some matters than the civil servant. This naturally leads on to the relationship of the civil servant to Parliament of which more anon, but Sir William Harcourt's famous dictum, 'The Minister exists to tell the civil servant what the public won't stand', is always to be borne in mind.

It has to be remembered that the Under-Secretary of today is perhaps the Cabinet Minister of tomorrow. I have known instances in the past where the permanent officials used to treat the Under-Secretary as of very little account. This is not a wise thing to do, for the young Minister must be trained and given responsibility if he is to grow up. Besides he may be the Minister of the future and a man of influence.

Every Minister naturally wants to get hold of the ablest civil servant for the headship of his department. If he is a junior departmental Minister he should look any gift horse presented to him by the Permanent Secretary to the Treasury very narrowly. He would be wise to consult his colleague under whom the postulant has served. He may, of course, be a brilliant and rising young man but, quite likely, he is a failure who is being passed on to the less experienced pending his welcome retirement.

On the other hand, a Minister should not be selfish. If there is a brilliant man coming on, he should not stand in the way of his promotion and transfer to another department, for the good of the whole must come first.

I was once asked what was the function of the civil servant in relation to the House of Commons. I replied that he sat in a dark seat under the gallery and listened to his Minister dropping bricks. But this is only part of the truth. The civil servant has to keep an eye on the House of Commons all the time.

I always consider that question time in the House is one of the finest examples of real democracy. One questioner may ask about world-shaking events, while another will ask why Mrs Smith of 5 Slum Alley, Coketown, was refused public assistance, or why the Post Office at Little Pedlington was closed last Friday. The effect of questions to the Minister and still more questions asked publicly in the House, is to keep the whole of the Civil Service on their toes. It is very seldom that any British civil servant is accused of rudeness or arrogance of the kind that is found sometimes in the *petit fonctionnaire* in other countries. At the time of writing the public mind is somewhat exercised over the Critchel Down affair. Undoubtedly, there was here a case where some civil servants failed to live up to the high tradition, but it should not be taken as typical. Indeed, the very fact of the interest aroused by this instance emphasized how exceptional it was. Complaint of arrogance or rudeness can always be made to the local member of Parliament. I believe that this is thoroughly salutary though it has a less useful side. It may induce in the civil servant a certain hesitation and nervousness in dealing with affairs. It may also lead to an overcentralization. This is due to the Permanent Secretary feeling too strongly the need for not embarrassing his Minister.

When I became Postmaster-General, I found what I considered to be an overcentralization in that office. Everything was channelled through the Permanent Secretary, Sir George Murray, and though this was partly due to the somewhat autocratic habit of mind of that distinguished public servant, it was also due to the fact that any minor mistake in the widespread network of the postal, telephone and telegraph services might be made the subject of a question in the House. As a matter of fact, I took certain steps towards decentralization and to a system of public relations. I might add that it was this fear of the effect on administration of detailed day-to-day Parliamentary supervision that was a factor in setting up public boards in nationalized industries instead of following the Post Office precedent.

A civil servant should rarely, if ever, be mentioned by name in the House, Everything that he does is the act of the Minister and it is the duty of the Minister to defend his servants and to take full responsibility.

Here comes in the need for Parliamentary experience. A Minister who has been long in the House understands its temper and what it will and will not take. Furthermore, he understands just what are the points on which his party feels strongly. This knowledge is necessarily outside the range of the official. Thus a neat and tidy scheme put up by a devoted civil servant may be technically correct, but it may not be acceptable to the House of Commons.

An example occurred when I was working with the late Lord Addison. A Bill was put up by a civil servant. As we were a minority government we expected to have difficulty in getting our legislation through. The ingenious official drafted a Bill with a minimum number of clauses on the ground that this would give few opportunities for long discussions on 'Clause stand part'. All the meat of the Bill was put into schedules. I had to point out that nothing annoyed members more than a Bill which was obscure and meaningless without constant reference to schedules. I redrafted it to make it simple and intelligible and, despite a larger number of clauses, it went through.

Equally, the Minister is more in touch with the ordinary man and woman than the civil servant. Something which seems quite reasonable to the middle-class professional may not go down with working people. I always found the late George Tomlinson a good touchstone in these matters. I would say: 'Well, what do you think of this, George?' He would answer: 'It looks all right, but I've been trying to persuade my missus about it for the last three weeks and I can't convince her.' It is the business of the Minister to bring in the common touch.

I expect that in his heart of hearts the civil servant thinks of Parliament as a necessary nuisance. He is liable to be called off from what he regards as more important work to search out the answer to some question which seems to him of little importance. The plan embodied in a Bill to which he has given so much work is likely to be altered in committee, probably, in his view, for the worse, while he is likely to waste a lot of time in the precincts of the House waiting for business which, after all, does not come on at the expected time. He may prepare an admirable note for his Minister on an amendment which is not called. Worse still, his Minister may have failed to understand it and may suffer humiliation at the hands of the Opposition while he sits impotently by. It may be, too, that, despite all his care in arming himself with every possible point of information, someone asks for some particular figures which he has not got, to the disgust of the agitated Parliamentary Private Secretary whom his Minister has despatched to seek light from 'under the gallery'. Sometimes, he has a sweet revenge when the persistent interlocutor of today is the Minister of yesterday and he is able to tell his Minister that action now so roundly condemned was in fact the work of that very man.

The civil servant, in dealing with the House, will find an invaluable assistant in the Parliamentary Private Secretary if he is worth his salt. He can often persuade a member to withdraw an awkward question or to arrange for a question to be put which will enable the Minister to show himself in a favourable light. The P.P.S. also knows what is going on in the House and can give timely warning that business which was thought to be going to take an hour is unlikely to last more than ten minutes, thus enabling the civil servant to avoid the disgrace of having his Minister absent when he should be in the House.

The civil servant soon learns that sufferance is the badge of all his tribe. He learns to expect more kicks than ha'pence. For some reason the press, for the most part, tend to regard him either as an idle parasite or as a meddling busybody. The first conception is no doubt a hangover from an earlier age when the happy beneficiaries of the patronage system fleeted the time merrily, but even today he is often thought of as a consumer of many cups of tea, enjoying a sheltered life. A certain type of business man is prone to regard the civil servant as someone who is battening on the community. He is one of 'a horde of officials'. All officials move in hordes. If he were doing precisely similar work for the business man he would become 'a valuable member of my staff'.

The civil servant must never defend himself publicly. That is left to his Minister, but if the latter does it, the journalist says: 'Of course, he has to defend his subordinates.' Nowadays the institution of public relations officers has done something to mitigate this hostility to officials, especially since the extension of Governmental activity has brought so many more in contact with officials who, generally, are both courteous and helpful. Here and there, as is inevitable, you do find the 'jack in office', but he is a rare bird.

When I was Postmaster-General, there was then a good deal of criticism of postal officials in the press and every little mistake was publicized, but later when I was able to arrange for some advertising of the telephone in the press there was a magical change.

There is one matter which causes some difficulty. Formerly, with few exceptions, the higher ranks of the Civil Service were filled by arts graduates. The specialist in science or technology was very rare, but nowadays progress of scientific inventions has meant that a different type of worker is required. But the competition for first-class scientific minds is intense and the ordinary Civil Service rates of pay compare unfavourably with what is offered in private industry. This inevitably sets up a strain in the administrative machine. The same difficulty may occur in relation to technicians or people from the world of business. In war the difficulty hardly arises but in peace-time it is very real and has not yet been solved.

I have said little here about the lower grades of the Civil Service though much of what I have said applies to them as much as to the administrative class. I am sure that some promotion is desirable as a stimulus. The Post Office sets a good example here for there are many instances of telegraph boys eventually arriving at positions of great importance. This, however, is part of the wider problems of recruitment and organization with which it is not my purpose to deal.

In general, the civil servant must be content with anonymity and obscurity until, in due course, his name appears in the higher categories of the birthday honours. Perhaps, after his retirement, he may become widely known. Every now and again there appears in the ranks of the Civil Service a bright star like Lord Waverley who shines brilliantly in a wider firmament but, for the most part, the civil servant must rest content with the consciousness of good work honestly done.

He may, at all events, feel that however modest his own achievements, he forms part of a service unequalled in all the world—one of the causes of a just pride in his fellow countrymen.

Chapter 3

THE REFORMS OF 1854 IN RETROSPECT

By The RIGHT HON. SIR EDWARD BRIDGES
G.C.B., G.C.V.O.
(Permanent Secretary to the Treasury)

LET us suppose that by some curious mischance all copies of the Northcote-Trevelyan Report had been lost, and that it had only been rediscovered in this centenary year of 1954: and that we could read it today for the first time. What effect would the report make on us?

We should be struck at once by its unlikeness to the blue book of today. It is far shorter—only some 23 quarto pages. And it is not written in the cautious, balanced manner of our present-day reports. Although the style is official, the tone is that of a man speaking with utter conviction in the absolute rightness of what he says: determined only to set out what he has to say as clearly as possible, and persuaded that once the truth and logic of his view was understood, it would certainly prevail.

Next, I think we should be impressed by the number of measures of first-rate importance contained in a small compass. And, springing from that, would come certain reflections. First perhaps that important as the measures are they have a certain obviousness. On that account we might tend for a while to underrate the report. But then we should recognize that the reason for this apparent obviousness is that all the important proposals in the report have long since been put into effect, and become part of the accepted, familiar order of things. And, last of all, it would be borne in on us that much of the character of the Civil Service of today derives to no inconsiderable extent from the Northcote-Trevelyan Report.

What were the main proposals in the report? (That is, perhaps, a more accurate expression than the convenient phrase 'The reforms of 1854'. For, as is well known, the report encountered strong opposition, and it was some twenty years before it could be said that much of it had been substantially adopted.)

The summary of recommendations in the report is in too general terms for our purpose. Stated broadly the main proposals were as follows:

First: a distinction should be established between intellectual and mechanical labour, and a separate system of recruitment should be set up for each.

Second: a central board of examiners should be established to conduct examinations for all candidates for the public service; periodical examinations being held on a Service-wide basis for the 'superior situations' (i.e. those corresponding to intellectual labour) and for mechanical labour; likewise examinations of a special character being held for posts calling for special qualifications.

Third: that for the 'superior situations' an endeavour should be made to secure the services of the most promising men of the day, by a competitive examination 'on a level with the highest description of education in the country'. This, it is made clear, is an attempt to secure first-class men from the universities.

Fourth: a group of proposals, not of special originality or importance, designed to secure that industry should be encouraged and merit rewarded.

Fifth: one of the main objects of the report was to combat what is described as 'the fragmentary character of the Service'. By this is meant what we should describe as 'excessive departmentalism'. To quote the report: 'Each man's experience, interests, hopes and fears are limited to the special branch of the Service in which he is himself engaged. The effect naturally is to cramp the energies of the whole body, to encourage the growth of narrow views and departmental prejudices. . . . ' The authors of the report looked to introduce into the Service 'some elements of unity' by the measures already described.

If one were to attempt to appraise the effect of each of these proposals separately, one would land oneself in confusion: for they were all part of a single scheme, devised to secure a more efficient public service. Nevertheless some comment is called for on individual parts of the scheme.

The separation of intellectual from mechanical labour strikes us today as remarkably obvious. It is a commonplace, beloved of every Establishment and Organization Officer (and rightly beloved) that when considering how any branch of work should be handled, the first step is to find out what qualities are called for from those who will be required, at different levels, to discharge the work. But this was far from being generally accepted 100 years ago. And yet its acceptance was the essential first step to securing opportunities for work of a character that could attract the university graduate.

The proposal to establish a central board of examiners—the Civil Service Commission—was hotly contested, but now has behind it 100 years of successful achievement. I shall make no attempt to describe its work in detail. But looking at the matter in a broader context, the setting up of the Commission did more than any other single factor to make the Civil Service into a truly public service. Until 1854 all appointments to the Civil Service owed something to patronage. Sometimes the patronage was exercised by a Minister, sometimes by the local M.P., sometimes by the departmental authorities. Often, no doubt, the patronage was administered disinterestedly: but the fact remained that those who entered the Civil Service under this system owed something to somebody's influence. All this was, before long, swept away: The Service became open to competition by all: a Service in which places were gained by merit and none owed his place to favour.

A special interest attaches to the aim of the report 'to mitigate the evils which result from the fragmentary character of the Service, and to introduce into it some elements of unity. . . . '

The Civil Service of this country has never been made the subject of a comprehensive statutory code.[1] Our Civil Service is departmental in its origins and has many strong departmental traditions. We have felt our way in the process of knitting the departmental staffs into a single service; and unifying influences have only been brought to bear stage by stage.

It is surely true to character (Trevelyan's logical and some-

---

[1] The conditions of service of civil servants are governed by statute only in respect of superannuation. The reason is believed to be that the first Superannuation Acts were passed to prevent undue liberality in awarding pensions in the era of patronage.

what ruthless character!) that the concluding paragraph of the report should express the 'conviction that if any change of the importance of those which we have recommended is to be carried into effect, it can only be successfully done through the medium of an Act of Parliament'. The words which follow make it clear that the authors of the report feared that their scheme, even if put into effect, would soon be eroded by strong departmental interest, unless it had behind it the force of law. But it was not to be. 'From time immemorial (wrote Sir James Stephen) the constitution of the Civil Service has been regulated by Royal Orders in Council.' The traditionalists had their way. And the Civil Service Commission was set up by Order in Council.

But, although the reforms of 1854 were not embodied in any Act of Parliament, nevertheless they mark the turning point between the 'fragmentary' period which had gone before and the beginning of a new cohesion, a slowly developing consciousness of unity in the Civil Service. The first essential in the process was the placing of first appointments to the whole Civil Service on a uniform footing under the control of the Civil Service Commission. This in turn had a powerful effect in bringing about a far greater uniformity of grading between posts in different departments; and such uniformity counted for a good deal, both in ironing out unnecessary differences which can easily cause friction between departments; and also in making it easier for staff to be transferred from one department to another.

In another way, recruitment from the universities proved to be a unifying factor, since it provided the Service with a succession of men capable of filling the highest posts, whether in their own or in some other department, and thus by degrees brought to an end what the report described as 'the system of appointing strangers to the highest offices' . . . and to 'the staff appointments'.

Northcote and Trevelyan were wrong in fearing that departmentalism would reassert itself and would wreck the report. Progress towards the unity of the Service may have been slow, but it was maintained.

The events of the last forty years have done much to foster the unity of the Civil Service. In two world wars new departments had to be set up, and old ones strengthened. Staffs for the purpose were drafted in large numbers from the departments less strongly pressed by war activities. And in the last decade or so, the economic climate has made it essential for all departments concerned with trade, finance or industry, to work together far more closely than ever before.

Again, for about the last 35 years, a system has been in force whereby the whole Civil Service has been the field of selection for the top posts in the Service; and it has usually been the case that nearly half the Permanent Secretaries started their official life in another department or had had a considerable period of service in another department.[1]

All these processes have helped towards a general realization that the whole matters more than the parts, and we have passed a long way from the 'fragmentary' period. But, looking back, it is fair to say that the setting up of a central system of recruitment was the essential first step in the development which has come about.

The last of the reforms on which I wish to comment—and probably the most important—was the proposal that the 'superior situations'—today we should say the administrative class—should be recruited from the universities.

It is worth pausing a moment to compare the extravagant things said in favour of this proposal, and against it, in 1854, with the grounds on which it was put forward in the report itself.

A most formidable array of educationalists supported the proposal with the utmost fervour, seeing in it a scheme which would stimulate and encourage university studies, by making it clear that success at the university was the main road of entry to a worthwhile profession.

The very ardour of the educationalists stimulated the opposition of those who, like Lord Robert Cecil (later Lord Salisbury) declared that the scheme was a schoolmaster's scheme, or agreed with R. W. Lingen, the Secretary to the Committee of the Privy Council on Education, who 'thought it quite beside the point to discuss the organization of the Civil Service as if it existed for

[1] In 1954 of 33 Permanent Secretaries of major departments, 16 started their official career in other departments and 4 others have spent long periods in other departments.

the sake of the general education of the country'. Critics from within the Service were not wanting whose attitude is illustrated by the view that 'something more than a high standard of education and varied information is needed in a junior clerk . . . '.[1]

Compare all this with the sober words of the report itself: 'To obtain first-rate men, it is obvious that recourse should be had to competition. It would be impossible to impose on each candidate for a clerkship, as a positive test of his fitness for the appointment, the necessity of passing an examination equal to that of first-class merit at the universities; but if, on the occurrence of a vacancy it is found that a number of candidates present themselves, of whom some are capable of passing such an examination, there can be no reason why the public should not have the benefit of such men's services, in preference to those of persons of inferior merit.'

In other words—'You want the best men; therefore you should take the best men from the universities, if you can get them.' The missing premise in the argument is filled in by the later statement that 'the examination would elicit young men of general ability, which is a matter of more moment than their being possessed of any special requirements'.

This, I am sure, is a true judgment; and I have no doubt that it would be generally agreed that what is now called 'university entry' to the Civil Service has been an outstanding success; and that it has provided the Civil Service with a succession of first-rate administrators.

But the matter goes deeper than that. There is, surely, a fairly close affinity between the qualities developed in the universities and those needed in the Civil Service. In both, you have to cultivate the capacity to analyse complicated situations, and to set out the results clearly and accurately. You cannot do that unless you have an inner determination to find out the right answer at all costs: unless you are always on your guard not to allow yourself to be swayed by the preconceptions or prejudices which we all have about any subject, before we have really studied it. Above all, you must not allow your sympathies to get entangled with what looks like an ingenious and satisfactory solution to your problem, before you have finished your collation

[1] See 'Civil Service Reforms, 1853-5', by Edward Hughes, published in *History* for June 1942 and reprinted in *Public Administration*, spring 1954.

and analysis. You must be ready to accept an awkward fact which shows that you have been on the wrong lines, and to start all over again.

As I see it, both in academic life and in the Civil Service you need this combination of intellectual integrity with the ardour of the chase. Moreover this combination of qualities has been of value to the Civil Service in another way. It is the pride of the Civil Service that it is non-political, and that it can serve Governments of all parties with equal loyalty and obtain their confidence. And this confidence is, perhaps, the more easily obtained by a Civil Service whose general attitude is slightly detached and withdrawn.

One other aspect of university entry is worth a moment's reflection. The report decided in favour of picking the ablest young men available, and training them in the Service rather than taking them from the professions. They assumed, too, that provided the competitive examination produced men 'equal to first-class men at the universities', it did not matter whether the subjects of the examinations had any relevance to the work done in the departments. Have the assumptions which underline this policy been justified?

This is too old and too big a subject for dogmatism. Let me shelter behind others. I believe that the general verdict of the Civil Service would be that they have been abundantly justified. But this does not mean that the Civil Service underrates the value of what George Arbuthnot, Auditor of the Civil List and one of the objectors to the report, spoke of when he said the 'humble and useful duty . . . (of civil servants) is by becoming depositories of departmental tradition . . . to keep the current business in due course. . . .' Much of the work of Whitehall depends, indeed, on funds of special knowledge which each department has acquired on its own subjects. But such knowledge can be acquired, maintained and refreshed without any individual civil servant being condemned to spend a lifetime in a single branch. Indeed much of the most valuable administrative experience (though of a rather different kind) is that which is obtained by those who spent their service in a succession of different tasks, and it is those who come to the Service with the best trained minds who learn most from this wider experience.

Looking back over the last hundred years, the reforms of 1854 have stood the test of time. What of the future? Do the qualities on which Northcote and Trevelyan based their Report provide sure foundations for the Civil Service of today? Does the Report provide guidance to those who are concerned with the administration of the Civil Service in the middle of the twentieth century? Let us look at some of the main changes which have taken place.

The Civil Service of today is of course far larger than it was a hundred years ago and it is also charged with an infinitely wider range of duties. But some of the changes have been more significant than this.

One of the biggest differences lies in the very large scientific, professional and technical staffs now employed by the government. A hundred years ago I suppose that lawyers were almost the only professionals employed in government service in any number. Today nearly all the professions are represented, and the total number of persons in government service with higher professional or scientific qualifications is over 20,000. Unlike other civil servants, many of those in this group enter government service after professional training and experience in the outside world: and their links with their colleagues in outside professional employment are far closer than any links between civil servants in the administrative-clerical branches and any outside group. Moreover, special problems arise in gearing the professional branches, with their own specialized advice and technique, into the work of the administrative branches. Here is a whole group of problems wholly outside the scope of the report of 1854.

More significant perhaps is the change which has come about in the nature of the duties of the Civil Service, and which has brought civil servants to an increasing extent into much closer contact with the public.

This shows itself in many ways. One example is the work of the Social Service Departments, where large numbers of civil servants, often in the lower grades, spend their time in dealing with members of the public who seek information or redress about their benefits under the social security schemes. Much of the training introduced into the Civil Service in recent years pays special regard to the side of the civil servant's duties which involve contact with the public.

Another example is the increasing concern of the state in economic affairs. The duties of many civil servants in economic departments—including those in the higher posts—are largely concerned with problems of industry and commerce and necessarily result in much negotiation and discussion with business men, with the representatives of employers and employed.

A third example can be found in the acknowledged need for all government organizations to include a section charged with making clear, to press and public alike, the measures which the department takes, the services which it renders, and the reasons which lie behind policies.

In the result, the duties of the civil servant of today, whether in the higher or the lower grades, lie far less than formerly in the writing of minutes and memoranda in the safe seclusion of his office. Far more than before, he is called on to meet and discuss on behalf of his Minister with members of the public. He must be able to state a case clearly and with vigour. He must show himself alert and knowledgeable of his business: he must show understanding of the public's troubles. But at the same time he must never forget that he is the servant of the Minister, and that he has no authority for his actions save that delegated to him by his Minister.

Nor would it have escaped the notice of the acute observer of public affairs that, where a civil servant fails to give a good account of himself in some matter which attracts public attention, the doctrine of ministerial responsibility does not shield him from a measure of public blame.

Looking at the matter in the broadest way, the points which I have mentioned in the last few paragraphs seem to me to amount to this: that the task of civil servants today is not only changing somewhat in character, but is, on the whole, becoming rather more difficult. The civil servant must at all costs retain his impartiality and his objectivity in the handling of controversial questions. Only so can he retain the confidence of whatever political party may be in power. But this detachment from the heart of controversy can no longer be obtained simply by aloofness or withdrawal into the back-room. More than ever is it necessary for the Civil Service to recruit the right type of men and women for the tasks which they have to carry out: and this at a time when the competition with industry for recruits at all levels is keener than ever before.

To return to the Report. Any one seeking guidance in the handling of these changes in the character of the Civil Service will find little or no help in the Northcote-Trevelyan Report. And the reason is clear. The Report did not set out to be a bible for the Civil Service administrators for all time. It contains none of those rather grand yet vague philosophic utterances which are so often relied upon for support a hundred years later for propositions which it is safe to say never occurred to its authors. On the contrary it is a matter-of-fact, closely argued document, directed to proving a limited number of propositions and securing their acceptance. It seems to me sufficient tribute to the Report that those propositions were accepted and are still as valid today as they were a hundred years ago.

Chapter 4

RECRUITMENT TO THE CIVIL SERVICE

By SIR LAURENCE HELSBY, K.B.E., C.B.
(First Civil Service Commissioner)

THE Order in Council which established the Civil Service
Commission and appointed the first Commissioners was
made on 21st May 1855. A fortnight later the Commissioners
met formally for the first time, and within another four weeks
they held their first written examination, having gathered the
candidates together three days in advance to explain what they
were to expect. The Commissioners described their duties[1] as
'novel and important', and certainly no time was lost in starting
upon them. But from 1855 to 1870 these duties were little more
than to test by written examination the basic qualifications of
candidates nominated for junior posts by the public departments;
the departments continued to do their own initial recruiting to
junior posts, and to make all appointments to higher posts, by
the various methods of patronage. In the first five years about
a quarter of the 10,000 candidates nominated by departments
failed to pass these tests, mostly in spelling and arithmetic.
Occasionally a competitive element entered, when departmental

---

[1] 'And it is hereby ordered, that all such Young Men as may be proposed to be appointed to any Junior Situation in any department of the
Civil Service shall, before they are admitted to probation, be examined
by . . . the said Commissioners; and shall receive from them a Certificate
of Qualification for such situation.

'And it shall be the duty of the Commissioners, in respect of every such
candidate, before granting any such Certificate as aforesaid:

'1st. To ascertain that the candidate is within the limits of age prescribed
in the department to which he desires to be admitted;

'2nd. To ascertain that the candidate is free from any physical defect or
disease which would be likely to interfere with the proper discharge of his
duties;

'3rd. To ascertain that the character of the candidate is such as to qualify
him for public employment; and

'4th. To ascertain that the candidate possesses the requisite knowledge
and ability for the proper discharge of his official duties.'

35

nominations were more numerous than the permanent vacancies to be filled. On 6th July 1855 the Commissioners held their first competition when they examined three men for the post of clerk in their own office; but it seems likely that these three were government servants in other departments. The first open competition by public advertisement and examination was for eight writerships in the India Office in 1859; for these posts there were 391 candidates, and the *Daily News* records that at the end of the examination three cheers were given for the examiner.

Examinations had been coming into use long before 1855. Classified degrees by examination had been introduced at Oxford and Cambridge early in the century. Some government departments had been using elementary examinations for years, and even in the Treasury, the centre of patronage, some vacancies had been filled by examination for a time about 1834; by 1853 Northcote and Trevelyan reported that a dozen or more offices were requiring clerks to pass examinations before admission. In 1833 Macaulay, then secretary to the Board of Control for India, had advocated examinations for the selection of boys to go to India (though nothing was done till 1855). The principle of selection by examination was in accord with the social and educational movements of the time, and reflected the stirrings of the growing middle class against privilege. No other process of selection by merit would have been practicable at that time, and even today, despite criticism, the written examination has great advantages provided that it is designed to test powers of thought and reasoning and not merely knowledge of facts or of the opinions of others.[1] It need not surprise us that from 1870, when open competition was laid down as the basis of recruitment to the Civil Service, written examinations alone were used for another forty years. Jowett had strongly advocated a 'viva' as early as 1854; but the first use of interview was in 1909, when the managers of the new labour exchanges were selected by interview alone. It was not until after the first world war that the interview became established as part of the selection process

[1] Northcote and Trevelyan insisted that the examinations should 'be so conducted as to test the intelligence, as well as the mere attainments, of the candidates'. Although the Commission has followed this policy from the beginning, there have been lapses; nearly a century ago, for instance, a question was set: 'Give the dates of the following events . . . The Deluge.'

for one of the main classes in the Service, the administrative class. Interview was introduced into the examination for the executive class only after the second world war, and the clerical class is still filled by written examination only—partly because the numbers are so large that interviews would prolong the selection process unjustifiably.

The principle that selection of recruits for the general classes of the Civil Service should rely on a 'liberal education' (Macaulay's phrase), and not call for experience, was established at the outset and is still observed; and methods of applying the principle have changed only a little. At the lowest level, clerical assistants are chosen by means of short tests consisting of simple 'right-wrong' questions on arithmetic, spelling, meanings of words, etc. Such tests have a serious disadvantage—they offer no scope for positive ability, such as in clear expression; but they have the compelling practical advantage of speed.

At the middle levels, the clerical and executive class examinations follow the pattern of the standard public examinations taken in grammar schools. The Commission are sometimes asked why candidates for the executive class should take another examination similar to the General Certificate of Education at about the time when they sit for the G.C.E. itself. There are several reasons for this. There are nine G.C.E. examining bodies, and though the Secondary Schools Examination Council does exercise a real levelling influence, nobody would claim that their standards are so close that a strict order of merit could be based on them. Indeed these examining bodies do not publish marks; some inform the candidates how they are graded, some give confidential information to head teachers, but there is no system which allows results to be compared. School-leaving examinations in Scotland and Northern Ireland are conducted separately, and, particularly in Scotland, follow a rather different pattern from those in England. The Civil Service Commission, with a fixed number of vacancies open for competition, must arrange their candidates in an order of merit which can be seen to be just, so that the candidate who receives, say, the 100th vacancy is clearly distinguished from the 101st candidate, who is unsuccessful. In any case the G.C.E. is intended to be a qualifying examination, and to select candidates through it on a competitive basis would be a misuse, even if it were practicable.

At the highest level, recruitment to the First Division was introduced in 1872 by means of a written examination of university degree standard (on the model of the one which the Commissioners had been conducting for the Indian Civil Service since 1858), and continued in this form until 1914. From the outset a wide range of optional papers was offered, with the intention of providing equitably for the man whose studies had taken him off the beaten track. In 1874 Jowett was led to complain that 'a youth who knows little of many things learned at a crammer's will beat another far superior to him in solid achievement'. There was some substance in this, for no limit was placed on the number of optional subjects that could be taken, and candidates were led to offer as many as they could, and to cram for them, in the hope of adding marks to their total in spite of deductions for 'mere smattering'. Not until 1906 was a limit put on the marks to be gained in this way. Sir Warren Fisher, who failed in 1902, entered the Service in 1903 after working up extra subjects in the intervening year.

During the 1914–18 war recruitment was suspended. In 1917 a committee under the First Commissioner, Sir Stanley Leathes, produced a scheme of examination intended to ensure that recruits had a broad general education; for instance, every candidate had to take a modern language paper and also a paper in general science, and an additional modern language paper could be offered counting 100 marks over and above the fixed maximum of 1,800. The Leathes Committee firmly included an interview in their revised scheme (a royal commission of 1912 had tentatively suggested it), and laid down the lines of present policy by requiring it to be a test of alertness, intelligence and intellectual outlook, conducted not in matters of academic study but in matters of general interest 'on which every young man should have something to say'. The examination was resumed under this new scheme in 1925[1] (from 1919 recruitment to Class I had been by interview only, as part of the reconstruction arrangements); but the attempt to give a lead to the universities on broad general education proved a failure (though the prin-

---

[1] An attempt to resume recruitment by the normal method of full examination (with interview added) was made in 1921, but was abortive because departments were unwilling to provide vacancies for any but reconstruction candidates.

ciples now applied by the University College of North Stafford-
shire provide an interesting parallel), and the additional papers
were dropped in the late 'thirties. For many years, however,
optional subjects were given different weights; classics and
mathematics were always given high values, for instance, so
that students of these subjects did not need to go outside them
to obtain their maximum marks, while other subjects which
were commonly read for university degrees, such as English or
French or law, had lower values and students of one of these
subjects could not take the examination without working up
another subject. The examination now gives equal opportunities
to students in the main degree subjects. The Commission's
present view is that if there is any real difference in the sort of
man that different university faculties produce it is the business
of the interview rather than of the written examination to detect
it and allow for it; but this is only possible when the interview
has been accepted as an integral part of the competition, as it
has since 1919.

While the full First Division examination is still in use for
recruitment to the administrative class by what is known as
method I, since the second world war an alternative means of
entry (method II) has been developed. The misleading descrip-
tions 'country-house' or 'week-end' are sometimes applied to
this method; but in essence it is simply based on the interview,
though a much extended interview. In general a successful candidate by method I is expected to show at least second-class
honours quality in the optional subjects, to gain over half marks
in the compulsory subjects (essay, English, and general papers)
and a satisfactory interview mark (although the total mark
alone affects the final result, the strength of competition makes
it difficult for a candidate to succeed if he falls far short in any
of these sections). In method II all candidates are required to
have a degree with at least second-class honours; there is a
compulsory written examination in essay, English, and general
papers, closely corresponding to the compulsory papers for
method I, and in general more than half marks are required to
qualify for interview. Those who so qualify come, after a series
of tests, before a Final Selection Board which applies the same
standards as the interview board for method I. The difference
between the two methods is that in method I the interview

mark (maximum 300) is added to the marks for the written examination (maximum 1,000), while in method II the interview assessment is the final and only result, the written examination and university degree being taken into account in it.

The tests or extended interviews under method II were held at a house in the country shortly after the war, and candidates lived on the premises for three days; but now the tests are held in London and candidates attend from 9 till 6. The purpose of the Civil Service Selection Board, to give the directing staff their official name (a misleading name since they do not select), is simply to learn as much as possible about the candidates by means of group tests and single interviews, as well as written exercises, and to lay the results before the Final Selection Board as part of the evidence to be taken into account. Each candidate has three single interviews with three of the directing staff: one mainly intellectual, one mainly psychological, the third of a more general kind. All candidates are given tests to work out in groups of six or seven, watched by three of the staff; these tests raise problems of a kind which, though simplified, are akin to those met in the ordinary run of work in the Civil Service (acting as chairman and as member of committees, assembling information and working out a solution to a problem of policy, etc.). Intelligence and other written tests are also given. Although each candidate is interviewed by a psychologist, and each team of three directing staff includes one psychologist, it would be wrong to imagine that the assessment made by the Civil Service Selection Board is mainly psychological, except in so far as all assessment of human beings can be called psychological. The Commissioners, and the Civil Service Selection Board itself, regard their function as common-sense judgment of candidates in straightforward situations. The judgment is not, of course, formed in a vacuum; the candidates have spent three or four years at university, and longer at school, and confidential reports from their tutors and headmasters are the essential foundation of the whole process.

Method II was introduced experimentally for a ten-year period, which expires in 1957. The decision whether the twofold system of recruitment should be dropped or retained will depend in part upon follow-up inquiries about candidates recruited by the two methods, and there are questions of time and cost which must be considered also. Method II was undoubtedly successful in the early post-war years among more mature candidates with a good deal of achievement to their credit in the Forces or elsewhere, who would have found it difficult to take a written examination requiring intensive academic preparation. Whether it gives better results than method I, or different results, with candidates who are just graduating, with nothing behind them but school and university and perhaps two years' national service, is far more difficult to judge. Perhaps the most striking practical advantage of the method lies in the fact that the results (provisional until degree results are known) are out before the end of the summer term at the universities, whereas the method I results cannot be declared till the end of August.

If selection is based only on a liberal education, the Service must train its recruits in the skills that they will need to do their work. The clerical and executive classes are recruited for general duties, but some of the work which comes to them is semi-specialized; auditing is an obvious example. Some Commonwealth countries require their clerical and administrative civil servants to obtain professional or other qualifications, either before or after entry; in Australia they become accountants, and in S. Rhodesia many take the examinations of the Chartered Institute of Secretaries. But in this country the recruit is not normally expected to acquire externally the semi-professional skills needed for some work. The necessary training for such work is given 'on the job', and the work is considered part of the ordinary run to or from which people may be transferred at any time. For instance, audit and accounting (not of fully professional quality) form a considerable part of the duties of the executive class. In general, training in the Service (which is carried out by departments, with the guidance of the Training and Education Division of the Treasury which deals with matters common to the whole Service) takes two forms: a short general course giving recruits an idea of their department as a whole, and detailed training on the particular job by the immediate supervisor. Fairly long, organized training courses, for which staff are removed from the actual work, seem best to suit the needs of the specialized departments, where the policy and the details of the duties can be clearly seen and a career can be built up on them; for instance, in the lower grades of the Post Office, the middle grades of Customs and Excise (Assistant Preventive Officers), and the higher grades of Inland Revenue (H.M. Inspectors of Taxes). For the administrative class the problem is different: the recruit is not intended to become a specialist, and the object is rather to develop in him qualities of wisdom and judgment which can be brought to bear in any field of administration. There is no external course of training, as in some countries (France, for instance, gives administrators a three-year course at a central college; India and Pakistan give a one-year course, also at residential colleges). Some specific training in procedure there must be, and the Treasury run a central course designed to show how the functions of the administrative class fit into the general machinery of government. But more important is experience of a wide range of administrative work, serving under a number of experienced seniors who will help the recruit and allow him to take progressively more responsibility on himself. Later in his career he may be among the half-dozen civil servants sent to each three-month course at the Administrative Staff College at Henley, or the more senior officers who take part in a course at the Imperial Defence College.

A high proportion of those selected for the administrative class and the senior branch of the Foreign Service are still drawn from the universities of Oxford and Cambridge, as they were before the war; and it is sometimes suggested that this argues a failure to keep pace with the democratic trend in education. For instance, in 1953 there were 52 successful candidates for the administrative class. Of these, 26 were Oxford and 15 Cambridge graduates; five came from London University, five from Scottish universities, and one from Nottingham. But it is necessary to probe a little deeper to appreciate the significance of these figures. First, 17 of the 52 candidates were educated at public schools and 35 of them at grammar schools. Second, 12 of the 52 came from working-class homes, 17 from lower middle-class homes (small shopkeepers, insurance clerks, non-graduate teachers, etc.) and 23 from middle-class homes. Of the dozen recruits of working-class origin seven were educated at Oxford or Cambridge, and eight got first-class honours degrees. When analysed in this way, the figures lend no support to the suggestion that the higher levels of the Service tend to be recruited from a particular stratum of society. On the contrary, they appear rather to illustrate the extent to which university education has now become available to all young people of real ability, not least at Oxford and Cambridge, and to suggest that the Commission need not fear that emphasis on university education (e.g., as the criterion of eligibility under method II) will unduly restrict the field of choice.[1]

The general competitions held by the Civil Service Commission are designed to fill vacancies in a number of departments, and when the competition is over the successful candidates have to be allotted to particular departments. Most candidates have preferences, some concerned with the nature of the work and some with the place where it is to be done. In the administrative class the conditions of service are much the same in all departments and nearly all the posts are in London; and the recruit's own wishes depend in the main on his estimate of the interest of the work of particular departments. But although some candidates would find it hard to believe, work of true administrative quality has much the same interest whatever the subject with which it deals; and the subject is often not what the candidate thinks it is. Many have a keen and natural interest, for instance, in educational problems; but they do not always realize that an administrator in the Ministry of Education is more likely to deal with finance or buildings than with what is taught, and to deal with local education authorities rather than schools and teachers. In general the successful candidate goes to the department of his choice unless others higher in the order of merit have taken the vacancies available. In the executive and clerical classes, however, the main problem is not the type of work, but the location of the office where it is to be done. Most recruits live outside London (before the war most of them were in the London area) and do not want to come to London, for various reasons (the expenses are greater, mothers do not want their daughters to leave home, etc.). They therefore seek assignment to departments having provincial vacancies. The Commission take pains to find out where the departments' vacancies are and assign candidates to them strictly in accordance with their places in the

[1] A hundred years ago, Northcote and Trevelyan accepted it as self-evident that the field of choice was 'the youth of the upper and middle classes'.

table of results. But once a recruit is appointed in his department the Civil Service Commission have no control over his movements, and it sometimes happens that a candidate low on the list is appointed to a post in London but later transferred by his department back to his home town, while another candidate from his own school, higher on the list, is appointed to a post in another department in London and has to stay there.

The development of the use of the interview is, as the earlier part of this article has indicated, an outstanding feature of the selection of recruits to the Civil Service since the war. And this development is especially striking in relation to scientific and professional staff. Recruitment in this field has in recent years acquired a new importance and the Civil Service Commission have taken direct responsibility for it. Two additional Commissioners have been appointed to deal with this work; one in 1946 for the recruitment of scientists and their ancillaries, and one in 1947 for the recruitment of engineers, and later of allied professional classes such as surveyors, and the corresponding technical groups.

Although scientists had been employed in the Civil Service before the war, it was not until 1945 that the scientific classes[1] were established on an inter-departmental footing, in parallel with the general administrative, executive, and clerical classes. But the very nature of scientific work created special problems of recruitment. The Commission had to recognize that each of the posts for which a scientist was required had its own specific requirements. The qualities required in a physicist to be engaged on meteorological work or in the National Physical Laboratory were markedly different, in terms both of ability and temperament, from those required in a nuclear physicist. Nearly all posts in the Scientific Officer Class, and a large proportion in the Experimental, show this kind of individuality; and it was clear from the beginning that no form of written examination could reach the degree of analytical delicacy necessary to give workable results. The Commission therefore relied

---

[1] Scientific Officers are drawn from graduates with first or second-class honours degrees; Experimental Officers from those with the Advanced level of the G.C.E. or the Higher National Certificate, or lower degrees; Scientific Assistants from those educated to G.C.E. Ordinary level or the Ordinary National Certificate, with laboratory experience also.

upon the most flexible method of all, that of interview—interview not used, of course, as a *viva voce* examination, but as an occasion for summarizing what could be made known of a candidate's life-history and of considering into which specific niche in the service the individual candidate might be fitted. Over the past nine years this method has been developed so as to combine the principles of central recruitment with the special circumstances—the specific nature of the posts, the urgency of so many demands, the need both of speed and flexibility—of Government scientific work.

The professional classes, like the scientific classes, were put on a service-wide basis shortly after the war, and responsibility for recruitment to them assumed by the Commission. The corresponding sub-professional groups, including draughtsmen, were not reorganized until later, but now all permanent vacancies are filled by competitions conducted by the Commission. In this field a minimum professional or academic qualification and appropriate practical experience are stipulated. Thereafter selection is by interview only, though in certain competitions for which the entry is many times the number of vacancies to be filled, only the candidates whose experience is most appropriate to the duties to be performed are called to interview. The minimum qualification required of candidates for professional posts is normally associate membership of the appropriate professional institution or examination passes exempting the candidate from the institution's examination. When appointed, therefore, the recruit has attained or is about to attain full professional status, and the experience and training he requires after recruitment are in the application of his professional knowledge to departmental problems. But the Civil Service does also provide opportunities, notably in the engineering field, for unqualified recruits to enter the Service and to gain, after entry, the experience and further qualifications necessary to become full members of their profession. In certain departments, indeed, apprenticeships are available, so that a complete engineering training is offered within the Civil Service.

The technical grades and the different types of draughtsmen, all of whom work under professional direction, are selected in the same way as the professional officers. They are required to have some basic qualification such as a national certificate and a specified apprenticeship or period of training before entering the competition.

Apart from the general classes of the Service which are employed on similar work in many different departments, there is a wide variety of posts in particular departments. These range from inspectors of salmon fisheries to inspectors of ancient monuments, from housing managers to commanders of revenue cutters; from the assistant keepers in the British Museum or the Public Record Office, inspectors of factories or members of the National Agricultural Advisory Service to postmen and telephonists. At the lower end a written examination is still used, in the case of postmen, for example; but it is a short 'right or wrong' test which can be marked on the spot and is used as a guide in the interview which is held afterwards. Elsewhere the possession of certain qualifications or experience, such as a university degree or an agricultural diploma, is laid down as a minimum requirement, and replaces the written examination; and, as in the professional and scientific field, the interview has become the means of final selection.

Whatever the methods of selection, the ultimate test of any system of recruitment is: does it produce enough recruits, and of the right kind? Any answer to that question must be cautious, for it takes several years to find out for certain whether recruits have turned out to be the right people, not merely for the posts to which they were recruited, but for the higher ranks of their class and for the Civil Service as a whole. In the administrative class of the Home Service and the senior branch of the Foreign Service the competitions are now producing just enough suitable candidates to fill our vacancies.[1] Not all of them are as good as the best; but the leading industrial firms also find themselves unable to fill all their posts with exactly the type of person they are looking for. In the executive class the Civil Service has been getting recruits of good quality; at the upper school-leaving age of 18, while the universities take most of the best (over half of those leaving school at 18-19 now go to universities) there are still enough left for 300-400 vacancies in the Service, though competition from industry is now becoming strong. Only about

---

[1] But since this was written the 1955 competition for the administrative class has produced only about two-thirds of the number of acceptable candidates required.

two-thirds of the 3,000 or so annual vacancies in the clerical class are filled; the reason for this probably lies in the increased number of pupils staying at school after 16, and in the fact that apprenticeships, professional articles, etc., draw on those who do leave school. In the typing grades and the other sub-clerical grades recruits of good quality are very scarce: no doubt this is because the Civil Service, with its salaries built up on a career basis (low at first and increasing with length of service), with its Saturday morning work and the need to travel to central London, cannot compete in this market with local employers. In the professional field the Civil Service has gone short of recruits of certain types (doctors, statisticians, accountants, lawyers, etc.) and has been seriously short of some (especially engineers and surveyors). But engineers are scarce the world over (in Canada the national output is expected to be 2,000 short of the national need in each of the next two or three years), and for the rest the Civil Service is not seriously understaffed in comparison with the professions as a whole. In the scientific classes, most vacancies have been filled. Of all scientific talent short of the highest class, the service has probably attracted at least a fair share over the last ten years. Many of the very best scientists make their careers in academic life; but perhaps partly by the attraction of schemes of promotion for special merit in research, and of senior and junior government fellowships, the Civil Service has recently drawn in a reasonable share of recruits of exceptional ability.

Chapter 5

RECENT TRENDS IN
PUBLIC ADMINISTRATION

By WILLIAM A. ROBSON

I

THE increased functions of the state are one of the most commonplace facts of modern political history. Every text-book on government emphasizes the vast growth in the duties and responsibilities of public authorities today compared with a century ago. This is unquestionably true. Indeed, not only are most of the functions of government relatively new, but so, too, are a majority of the departments which carry them out.

In 1854, very few of the government departments which we know today had come into existence. The Treasury, Home Office, Board of Trade, Foreign Office, Post Office, Admiralty, Customs, Inland Revenue, Lord Chancellor's Department, and Office of Works, were the principal exceptions. The Ministry of Agriculture and Fisheries dates from 1903 (when the former Board of Agriculture and Fisheries was set up); the Ministry of Education from 1899 (if we take the Board of Education as its progenitor); the Air Ministry from 1917; the Ministry of Labour from 1917; the Ministry of Health from 1919; the Ministry of Supply from 1939; the Ministry of Fuel and Power from 1942; the Ministry of National Insurance from 1944; the Ministry of Housing and Local Government from 1951, or from 1943 if we regard the Ministry of Town and Country Planning as its progenitor. The Ministry of Transport was created in 1919 and the Ministry of Civil Aviation in 1944: the two were merged in 1953.

We can thus see that a substantial proportion of our major departments are of recent origin; and this is an indication in terms of structure of the enlarged scale and scope of government functions. But the proliferation of departments is by no means the only sign of expansion. The Ministry of Health, for example,

48

was before 1946 mainly engaged (apart from its special war-time tasks) in the work which now falls on the Ministry of Housing and Local Government. In 1951, it shed its other functions, and since then has been almost wholly occupied with the new national health service. The Home Office has recently had many new duties placed upon it in connection with the fire service, civil defence, and the care of deprived children needing help and protection. The functions of the Treasury, no less than its outlook, have changed greatly since 1939. It is concerned to a far greater extent than before with the co-ordination of economic policy, the full use of our productive resources, the balance of trade problem, general control over investment and capital development, and international economic organs (of which OEEC is an outstanding example). In short, the functions of the older departments have in some cases expanded and changed almost beyond recognition.

I am endeavouring to show that, in addition to an enlargement of the scale and scope of state action, the character of public administration has altered in certain important respects. It would be strange if this had not happened when one comes to consider the nature of the welfare state to which both the great political parties are now committed. For this means that the state is involved in new and difficult tasks. It must endeavour to avoid mass unemployment, to promote industrial peace, to ensure a high degree of social security, to control capital investment, to secure a favourable balance of trade, to obtain a rising standard of living for the mass of the people, to increase productivity, to redistribute wealth through taxation, to maintain a national minimum standard of life below which no one shall be permitted to fall.

Whatever government is in power will almost certainly—in the absence of war or economic disaster—develop in various ways the social services, particularly the five great groups concerned with health, housing, education, social insurance, and town and country planning.

The age of privilege is passing, the era of equality of opportunity is approaching. The traditional concept of freedom among the British people has been a negative one. It has signified freedom from the tyranny of the executive, freedom from arbitrary arrest and imprisonment, freedom from taxation without representation, freedom to carry on one's trade or to dispose of one's labour as one pleases, freedom of speech and of writing, freedom of association and of meeting. Now, in addition, we are seeking positive kinds of freedom through the instrumentality of the state. These include the opportunity for every man or woman to realize the maximum degree of self-fulfilment of which he or she is capable; the chance to participate in the cultural heritage of our civilization; the opportunity to climb the ladder according to one's ability without regard to birth or wealth; and a minimum standard of life below which no one shall sink.

The principles of equality, social justice, individual and communal well-being, embodied in the welfare state are expressed in practice through the manifold programmes, policies and activities of government departments, local authorities, public corporations and other public bodies. This article deals only with government departments but one must remember that they do not work in isolation from these other organs.

II

The fundamental principles of the welfare state have greatly changed the work of public administration. The older regulatory functions, typified by the Factories Acts, which require officials to apply and enforce detailed legislative provisions controlling the conduct of particular categories of persons of establishments, have become less prominent than service functions, in which the government provides a service either in cash or in kind for the individual or for the whole community. Medical treatment given under the national health service, training and rehabilitation courses offered to persons suffering industrial injuries, the vocational guidance given to boys and girls leaving school, the jobs found for disabled persons, sickness or unemployment benefit, houses provided by local authorities and subsidized by the state —these are a few examples of service functions in cash or in kind provided by the welfare state.

Although the major emphasis is now on service functions, many new kinds of regulatory functions have recently appeared. Town and country planning is a regulatory service of the highest importance, but it differs from the older regulatory services in that the controls it imposes are incidental to the realization of planning policy and specific development plans.

Many departments have much more positive and creative tasks to perform nowadays than was formerly the case. The Ministry of Labour and National Service, for example, was mainly engaged before 1939 in administering unemployment benefit and the placement of manual workers. Today it is largely concerned with deploying the labour force to the best advantage, having regard to the needs of the Forces, industry and other occupations. It is responsible for national service, demobilization, and reinstatement in civil employment. It enrols and allocates persons with managerial, executive, and technological qualifications, and tries to forecast the future demand for scientific and technical personnel. It plays a much larger part in the sphere of industrial relations and in avoiding stoppages of work. It attempts to supply labour shortages by bringing immigrants to this country from abroad.

The Board of Trade is another department which is engaged in some very different tasks from those which occupied it in the past. It is the principal department for controlling the location of industry, and no new factory (above a minimum size) can be built in any part of the country without the approval of the Board. One of the most constructive jobs it has done since 1945 has been to build up the so-called Development Areas (formerly known as the Depressed Areas) by guiding to them many different kinds of factories and other forms of productive enterprise. The investigation and control of monopolies is another new function of the Board of Trade.

The great increase in international organization since the end of the second world war has affected the work of several departments. The activities of the International Civil Aviation Organization (ICAO) affect the administration of the Ministry of Transport and Civil Aviation in respect of air services, ground services, international agreements, and many other matters. The Ministry of Education plays an active part in relation to Unesco, and the Ministry's external relations branch also has many working contacts with education authorities in the Commonwealth and foreign countries. The Ministry of Health has relations with the World Health Organization and must take account of it in its domestic administration from time to time; the Ministry of Agriculture has relations with F.A.O., and so on. The work of the Foreign Office is far more deeply affected by the United

Nations than it was by the League of Nations. Before the war, the Ministry of Labour and the Post Office were the only departments seriously affected by the work of international organizations. Today, international organs make an impact on the work of many departments.

Science occupies a much larger place in the sphere of government than in the past. This applies both to the civil and the service departments. Leaving aside such spectacular events as the development of atomic energy, for which the Ministry of Supply was until recently entirely responsible, we may observe that the aircraft side of that Ministry is concerned largely with scientific research and development, some of it carried out in government establishments like the Royal Aircraft Establishment, some of it by firms making aircraft or engines, some of it by universities. The Mines Department of the Board of Trade had not the slightest inkling of the meaning of research or development, and the same was true for some years of its successor, the Ministry of Fuel and Power. Today, that department has a scientific staff of high calibre which is influencing its policy and administration in various ways. The promotion of research relating to agriculture, horticulture, and fisheries has become an important part of the work of the Ministry of Agriculture and Fisheries, while the National Agricultural Advisory Service acts as a link between farmers and research establishments.

In the second world war much closer relations developed between government departments and business than had previously existed at any time. Close relations continued during the two post-war Labour Governments, partly because of the grave economic difficulties which faced the country and partly because the government was determined as a matter of policy to continue control over such matters as building licences, capital development, and the import and export programmes. The relations between government and business are possibly less close today but they are certainly closer than before 1939, and they are likely to remain so. The Regional Boards for Industry, composed of senior regional officers of several ministries and representatives of industry, commerce, and trade unions, which were set up during the war, have remained in existence with advisory functions in their respective regions; while at the national level the National Production Advisory Council for Industry still considers questions of general interest relating to industry and trade under the chairmanship of the Chancellor of the Exchequer. Questions of man-power and labour are discussed by the National Joint Advisory Council presided over by the Minister of Labour. By these and other means an increasing number of civil servants are brought into contact with business men and industrialists in the course of their work. Mutual understanding and good relations are of the first importance.

Another big change in the work of public administration is the new emphasis laid on development. Of course it is true that this country, like many others, has been developing its resources for centuries. But both rulers and citizens have been far more aware of the need for development since 1945 than before the war; and government has recently assumed new responsibilities for development in several spheres. For example, there is the unprecedented effort at building 14 or 15 new towns. The development corporations appointed under the New Towns Act are primarily responsible, but it is a Minister who appoints them and chooses the site; who has to provide them with money and see that it is properly spent; who must approve the plan for the new town; and assist and supervise the corporations in many different ways. Moreover, many other government departments are involved in the provision of services required by the new towns.

The Colonial Office must be full of civil servants whose main watchword is development: for economic, political, and social development has become the essential core of British colonial policy in recent years. This is one of the reasons why, in addition to being organized in geographical departments, the Colonial Office has a series of functional departments concerned with many different questions which arise in connection with development, such as production and marketing, civil aviation and communications, social services, commercial relations and supplies, and advice on research.

Lastly, public administration today demands as never before a high degree of communication between the governors and the governed. The classical theory of democracy postulated a representative legislature based on a popular franchise to make the laws, a responsible executive to carry them out, and an independent judiciary to see that everyone, including public authorities, observed the law. The rôle of the citizen was limited to casting his vote every few years, and he then faded out of the picture in a cloud of satisfaction with his handiwork.

It is now realized that the citizens must play a much more active part if government is to be efficient and democracy to succeed. The speeches of Ministers and Parliamentary debates must be reinforced at the administrative level by a constant stream of two-way communication between government departments and the public. If departmental policies and programmes are to be accepted and to work effectively they must be explained to those concerned. Where the active co-operation of citizens is required in, for example, an immunization campaign against dipthheria, or an effort to reduce road accidents, or a drive to increase savings, or to avoid a slump by spending more, or an effort to achieve more hygienic methods of handling food, not only must the aims and methods adopted by the department be carefully explained but the public asked to respond in a particular way. The public should be kept regularly informed of what departments are doing or trying to do, the results they have achieved, the difficulties they have encountered, the shortcomings they have experienced and also the mistakes they have made —frankness and the acknowledgment of error is a sign of strength, not of weakness. On the other hand, the departments need to receive constant information from the public as to how their administration is working from the citizen's point of view, what are its effects, what improvements might be made, where the shoe pinches.

The modern need for communication has resulted in information or public relations officers being appointed in the Prime Minister's office and in all government departments, and to press attachés or information officers being a normal feature of every embassy or high commissioner's office. It has produced the Central Office of Information, the Economic Information Unit in the Treasury, and the amazing range of publications of H.M. Stationery Office (of which we may be legitimately proud, for they represent an unrivalled level of achievement). It has produced the social survey as a frequently used device for discovering not only facts but attitudes, wishes, dislikes and opinions. It has led to the setting up of a large number of advisory committees on which disinterested 'laymen', or outside experts or representatives of special interests, trades or occupations are invited to serve, in order that their knowledge, experience, and views may be taken into account by government departments in dealing with a wide variety of subjects. Broadly speaking, while certain aspects of communication are entrusted to information officers and other specialists, a recognition of the basic need has in many ways influenced the work of large numbers of civil servants of all classes.

We may briefly summarize the principal changes which have affected the nature of public administration in recent decades by saying that civil servants are much more closely concerned than formerly with economic matters, with labour relations, and with negotiations with industrial and commercial bodies; they are required to have a more positive and constructive attitude to their work, and to undertake or formulate planning and development policies in many spheres; they are brought into contact with international organizations, or must take them into account, to a far greater extent than formerly; the rôle of the scientist, and of scientific research and development, in public administration has enormously increased; and finally, the need to establish and maintain constant communication with the public is recognized to an unprecedented extent.

III

We may ask now certain questions of great moment about the Civil Service. The first is whether the methods of recruitment now in use are well adapted to take into account the present needs of public administration. My own view is that, although a great advance has been made by the introduction of method II for admission to the administrative class, there is still room for further improvement.

The great merit of method II is that instead of examining the purely intellectual qualities of candidates by setting them written papers calling for the sort of knowledge and mental ability demanded by an honours degree in a British university, the Civil Service Selection Board tests the candidates' potential working ability in dealing with hypothetical administrative problems. The tests are designed to reveal temperament and personality as well as quality of mind. They demonstrate a candidate's powers of leadership, ability to co-operate, alertness in grasping a situation, quickness in assimilating relevant facts, lucidity and persuasiveness in presenting a point of view, ability to understand the administrative or political implications of a problem, resourcefulness in solving it, capacity for team work and good fellowship. They disclose intellectual power *in action*, and they make it possible to distinguish the man or woman of constructive outlook from the negative, indifferent, or sceptical type. They permit a much nearer approximation to a judgment of the whole man than the old-fashioned style of written competitive examination which is still used for the recruitment of the larger proportion of the administrative class and the entire clerical and executive recruitment.

I must qualify this warm tribute to the merits of the new type of examination by suggesting that still greater benefits might result from method II if the Civil Service Commission were to analyse in greater detail than they have so far done the qualities of mind and temperament required for different types of administrative work. When CSSB was set up in 1945, one of its first tasks was an attempt to formulate the qualities and characteristics required of candidates for the higher Civil Service and Foreign Service. For this purpose a survey was made of the work done by Assistant Secretaries in various government departments. The results of this survey of the duties of about 500 Assistant Secretaries were then classified under three main headings as follows[1]:

A. *Policy matters:* Discerning the more important general questions and problems arising out of the work of the Branch; seeing their implications, for the future as well as for the present, and for the country as a whole as well as for the department; formulating practicable, and, if necessary, detailed proposals for action; foreseeing the probable results of such proposals, including their effect on public opinion; taking responsibility, when required, for their adoption and organizing and supervising their execution.

B. *Paper work:* Analysis of complicated material, including figures, and accurate and cogent presentation of results; writing clear, brief, informative and acceptable letters and minutes.

C. *Personal contacts:* Discussing in committee, in conference or tête-à-tête for the purpose of reaching a decision, putting a

[1] Memorandum by the Civil Service Commissioners on the use of the CSSB in the Reconstruction Competition. H.M.S.O. 1951 p. 8.

point of view, or obtaining information; controlling subordinate staff; briefing superiors; negotiating with and representing the policy of the department to individuals or organizations outside the Service.

This simple triad of duties collected from a survey covering virtually the whole range of government departments and a number of British diplomatic missions abroad, has been treated as a sufficient job analysis on which to base the selection of suitable candidates and the devising of tests by which they can be discovered.[1] In my opinion it is quite inadequate because it fails to distinguish sufficiently between different departments or between different kinds of work. A distinction is drawn between the Foreign Service and the Administrative Class; and for the former the tests appear to be guided mainly by a desire to select candidates with 'a balanced personality', whatever that vague notion may mean.

This is not nearly good enough. Psychological analysis of different types of government work would indicate the qualities of mind and personality required for diplomacy, for negotiation or conciliation, for planning and development, for work involving contact with underdeveloped peoples, for personnel administration, for finance and accounting, for work involving frequent intercourse with business men, farmers, industrialists, and so on. I have a strong belief in the virtues of the administrative, executive, and clerical classes as general grades to be found in nearly all departments. I do not for a moment want to break up the administrative class into a series of specialist groups. But it is quite unrealistic to assume that all administrative work at any specified level is of much the same kind and to recruit candidates on the assumption that they will all be able to perform efficiently this hypothetically uniform work. A civil servant's work varies not so much according to the subject-matter of his department as according to the character of the function in which he is engaged. It follows therefore that the Civil Service Commission or CSSB and the departments should embark on a more profound study of job-analysis than they have so far attempted and then relate the working tests, interviews, and written tests in the method II examination to the results on

[1] It. p. 9.

a more differentiated basis. Method II, perhaps in a simplified form, might also be applied to the executive class entrance examination, and perhaps even to the departmental classes.

My second question relates to training. I adhere to the traditional view that it is right to recruit the brightest graduates from the universities for the Civil Service, irrespective of the subjects they have studied. I believe, however, that the social sciences can be of unique value in assisting a civil servant to understand the social, economic and political background of his working environment. Members of the administrative class, in particular, and at least some of the professionals, the lawyers, the doctors, the scientists, the statisticians, should in their early years be given an opportunity, or even be required, to take courses for the Diploma of Public Administration at one of the universities, if their previous education has left them completely ignorant of economics, political science, social history, sociology, social psychology, and so forth.

Despite the flutter caused by the Assheton Committee's report on training in 1944 (Cmd. 6525) our central training arrangements are very weak. Departmental training varies so much that it is difficult to generalize. But very little is still done for the younger members of the administrative class or for the professional and scientific classes who are of mounting importance. Assistant principals attend short intensive courses at the Treasury lasting two or three weeks, where they hear occasional lectures by other civil servants on selected topics—never really getting to grips with anything. We have nothing to compare with the *Ecole Nationale d'Administration* in Paris, with its three-year course of training for the new entrant to the higher cadres, or even the Indian Administrative Training School at Delhi with its one-year course. The time has come when a central training school for the administrative, professional and scientific classes, and perhaps the technical and executive classes, should be established.

IV

Lastly, more attention should be given than hitherto to the 'linked experience' of the civil servant's career. Experience may be regarded as a part of training—the part which goes on all through one's active life—or as something distinct from training.

But whichever view one takes of that, there is much to be said for enabling civil servants to gain relevant experience in the course of their official careers. This means: first, that a deliberate effort should be made to see that at least the higher and middle civil servants obtain experience in a number of different departments, instead of the matter being left largely to chance, as it is at present. Apart from war-time, it is surprising how often one meets civil servants who have served 20 years or more in one department. This cannot be to the public advantage or favourable to a unified Service.

At the same time one knows of civil servants who have moved about widely and frequently in the Service, without any connecting link between their posts being visible. The man who goes from a War Office supply centre overseas to a job in the Ministry of Agriculture and Fisheries concerned with giving grants to farmers engaged in hill farming may be having an agreeable change—and one wants to save civil servants from boredom or monotony—but his public usefulness may be reduced rather than increased by the transfer. The theory of the universal horizontal interchangeability of the Treasury classes is not really well founded amid the tremendous complexity and specialization of government departments today.

One course would be to group departments into such categories as those dealing with economic matters, social services, defence, overseas countries, etc., and to arrange for civil servants to circulate among the departments comprising the group to which they belong.

I admit that this would only produce relevance of experience as regards the subject-matter of the department's functions. I should therefore also favour interchange between groups where some degree of relevance can be attained in the particular appointments. We do not want to consign a civil servant to a specialized type of job, say finance or establishment work, for life—Heaven forbid. Change can be fruitful. But more regard should be paid than at present to the idea of increasing the civil servant's usefulness by extending his relevant experience—the emphasis is on relevant. One knows of senior officials appointed late in life to very high posts utterly remote from their previous experience. Sometimes they are sufficiently gifted to rise above their own ignorance in a fairly short time. But in other instances it takes several years before they have learnt enough to be of real use—and they are then due to retire. We could avoid such costly mistakes as these by planning the careers of our civil servants with more care and more regard to the difficulty of mastering in a few weeks or months the complex and technical problems which confront the senior officials in many departments today.

An administrator of genius will always find a way to do great things, despite unfavourable circumstances. We scarcely need to trouble about him, for he will flourish no matter what handicaps may exist. He is doubtless to be preferred to a man of lesser ability, even if the latter has had a more relevant experience in his official career. But the really outstanding administrator of unmistakable quality is comparatively rare even in the Civil Service; and we can assist and improve the efficiency of the rest by the sort of arrangements suggested above.

The Civil Service is one of the most valuable possessions of the British nation. We can best show our appreciation of its merits by a continuous effort towards its improvement. Much has been done since 1945 to modernize the Service, but further reforms are needed. The purpose of this essay is to show that we must not assume that the tasks of the Civil Service, or of any particular part of it, remain constant for indefinite periods of time. Public administration has changed greatly in our own day and it is likely to go on changing. Those who are responsible for the Civil Service, whether as Ministers, members of Parliament or senior officials, should do their utmost to discern and interpret the emerging changes in good time so that today's reforms really are designed to meet the needs of today and tomorrow, and not those of yesterday or the day before. The great merit of Trevelyan and Northcote was that they were looking forward to the future and not backward to the past. We should emulate them in this respect.

Chapter 6

THE FOREIGN AND COMMONWEALTH SERVICES

By ERNEST DAVIES, M.P.
(Under Secretary of State for Foreign Affairs, 1950-1951)

THE Foreign Office and Diplomatic Service has long been regarded with prejudice. Its necessary adherence to convention and tradition, its strict observance of protocol, the narrow social circle from which it was drawn and the maintenance in embassies abroad of standards of diplomatic life quite out of keeping with modern ideas are among the reasons. Belief that it is the Foreign Office rather than cabinets and Ministers that make foreign policy is another reason why it is looked at askance. This is mistaken prejudice. The Foreign Office does not comprise only gentlemen of means, drawn from Eton and Harrow and Oxford and Cambridge, well versed in culture and social etiquette, but less so in commerce and economics. Nor does the Foreign Office determine policy; for that the Prime Minister and Secretary of State are responsible, and the Cabinet and Parliament have the last word.

In all these regards there have been great changes during the last century. Transformation began with the merging of the Foreign Office and Diplomatic Service after the first world war and was completed with the 1943 reforms which added the Consular and the Commercial Diplomatic Services and brought them together into a unified Foreign Service distinct from the Home Civil Service.[1] Partly because of this and partly because the work of the Foreign Office has greatly increased, the total staff has trebled since 1939, and now exceeds 8,000 including the locally recruited staff but excluding the German section of about 1,000. The Foreign Office personnel in branch A (which is referred to later) is approximately only 700.

When the Foreign Office first became a separate department

[1] Proposals for the reform of the Foreign Service 1943 Cmd. 6420.

in 1782 the Secretary of State and his Under-Secretaries did most of the work themselves and it was not until 1906 that Sir Eyre Crowe introduced reforms which led to the establishment of a modern office responsible for the preliminary sifting and assessment of incoming information, tendering advice and drafting outgoing instructions. Equally casual was recruitment. Until the establishment of the Civil Service Commission in 1855 entrance into the Foreign Office was by nomination only and not until 1870 was competitive entry instituted.

The Diplomatic Service is of as ancient vintage as many of its surviving customs. Ambassadors originally chose their own staff who had to have private means. It was not until 1883 that nepotism was curtailed and entrance became competitive. Even then private means were still essential and up to the end of the first world war anyone entering the service had to guarantee that for the first two years he would support himself at the rate of £400 a year. The Consular Service was separately recruited and was not modernized until 1903 when competitive entry was started, and grades were introduced, The Commercial-Diplomatic Service dates from the end of the 1914-18 war when the Department of Overseas Trade was created. The Information Services were added after the last war on the dissolution of the Ministry of Information.

Reform was long overdue. The fault of the Service lay not only in the narrow though widening circle from which it was drawn, but also in the division of function between so many separate services; disparity between conditions of service at home and abroad caused a lack of flexibility that affected the efficiency of the Service. But the main need for change was the failure of the Foreign Service to keep abreast of modern development. Economic affairs had become as important as political, and commercial as social. Although the academic achievement of members of the Service was distinguished, a first-class honours degree being almost essential, those successful in entering the Service were more likely to be trained in classics or English than in economics or political science. The fusion of politics and economics in foreign affairs, which characterized the twentieth century, demanded certain qualifications, and it became desirable to open the Service to all possessing them, irrespective of social or scholastic background, and to make all posts available to every member of the Service. This required new methods of recruitment and training and a simpler procedure for weeding out the misfits.

The amalgamation of the services makes possible free interchange between posts of different type and thereby provides greater opportunity for variety of training and experience, enlarges the field of selection, facilitates choice of the right type for each specific assignment, and offers greater opportunity for promotion to the highest posts in the Service. Further, the establishment of the Foreign Service as a separate but unified section of administration made possible a freer inter-change between service at posts abroad and in the Foreign Office in London. Previously, conditions at home were closely assimilated to those of the Civil Service and were so disparate from those abroad that this had been difficult. As a consequence, representatives abroad were in danger of becoming expatriates, out of touch with conditions in the country they represented. Since the reforms, all become equally liable for service in the Foreign Office or at a mission abroad and provision is made for special allowances to compensate for any financial disadvantages that arise from transfers from post to post. The intention is that all shall periodically have a spell of duty in London, and by and large that is now carried out although it is not always possible at the highest levels.

Changes in method of recruitment and training were necessary to meet the changed character of the Service. Previously a candidate entering the Foreign Service had to appear in front of a selection board before he could even enter the examination. The result was that social qualifications ranked high and had to be satisfied before academic ability was proved. The examination was stiff, and possibly resulted in an over-intellectualization of the Service; certainly the emphasis was wrongly placed. A further disadvantage of the former system was that the standard of the written papers was so high that they could not be taken without intensive and specialized cramming which for many necessitated language study abroad at private expense. As this debarred those without time and funds for such education, it constituted an additional obstacle to the democratization of the Service. The present system reverses the order of selection and examination.

The new unified service is organized into four sections known as branches A, B, C, and D, of which branch C comprises the lower clerical grades and branch D the established chancery messengers and similar staff serving abroad. Branch A is the equivalent of the administrative grade of the Civil Service and consists of higher officers holding the Queen's commission. Entry is open to all between $20\frac{1}{2}$ and 24 years of age holding a first or second class honours degree and is by open competitive examination arranged by the Civil Service Commission. For those not so qualified a more comprehensive examination is held. Successful candidates for branch A then go through the ordeal of personal selection. For three days, in company with their fellow victims, they are under practical examination and observation by their selectors ending with an interview with the Final Selection Board which sits under the chairmanship of the First Civil Service Commissioner. Its members include representatives of industry, the trade unions and universities, civil servants and active and retired members of the Foreign Service. Although this system is similar to that of selection for the Higher Civil Service it has frequently been criticized in its application to the Foreign Service, particularly when the personal selection took place outside of London and the process was ridiculed as a glorified country house party. It has distinct advantages providing as it does an opportunity for judging the suitability of candidates successful in the examination for the unique requirements of the Foreign Service. It also permits of greater flexibility in selection. Personality, temperament and sociability cannot be written off as unimportant in a potential ambassador. Some candidates may not be examination-minded and may fail to obtain the requisite marks but come near enough to justify a chance at the Civil Service Selection Board, before which they may reveal just those qualities which are required for successful representation abroad. The reverse is also true because those most successful academically and adept at examination may prove to be morose introverts who hardly make the best ambassadors. A few older persons, from 20 to 30 a year, are recruited from time to time on the basis of past qualifications and activity. This enables people with experience in other departments or services, as for instance, the Indian Civil Service or the armed forces, to be brought in. Selection is again by the

Civil Service Commission but there is no competitive examination, only interview, and there is a relaxation of the academic qualifications.

Recruits for branch B, which corresponds roughly to the executive and clerical classes of the Home Civil Service, are drawn by open examination from the $17\frac{1}{2}$ to 19 years of age group for the executive classes and the 16 to 18 age group for the clerical. There is opportunity for advancement from branch B to branch A. For both branches there is provision for language specialization and vocational training which frequently take place abroad. All successful candidates in both branch A and B are on probation for three years.[1]

The main purpose of recruitment on the basis of open competition was to widen the catchment area and to bring into the Foreign Service a more representative cross-section of the community. An analysis of the scholastic history of the post-reform recruits shows that some progress has been made. The 351 new entrants into branch A between 1945 and 1954 inclusive came from no fewer than 163 different schools, while five were privately educated. A little under two-thirds, or 251, came from Headmasters' Conference schools, but only 36 from Eton and 4 from Harrow. Winchester contributed 28, Stowe 15, and Rugby 13. A number of the lesser public schools figure in the list including Manchester Grammar, five, Merchant Taylors, four, and St. Paul's Boys, three. The net being widely cast has resulted in a diversity in pre-university education but the same is not true of the universities. The vast majority graduated from the two older universities. 181 came from Oxford, 120 from Cambridge and only 15 from London. Edinburgh and Glasgow sent five each, St. Andrews two, and Aberdeen one. New Zealand universities contributed four, Irish two, and Vienna one. The red-brick universities were represented only by Liverpool and Southampton, which sent one apiece. Thirteen had no university education. While, therefore, it is still true that the vast majority of new entrants to the Foreign Service went from public school to Oxford or Cambridge, no one public school predominated. Nor, perhaps, should the older universities be regarded in the same light as before the reforms, since nowadays

---

[1] For a detailed account of recruitment and conditions of service see *The Foreign Office*, by Lord Strang Ch. IV and V.

more than 70 per cent of the undergraduates are state aided and both Oxford and Cambridge tend to provide the academic training which qualifies them for the Foreign Service rather than the newer universities which specialize more in technical subjects. On the other hand, the Foreign Office makes no special attempt to attract graduates from the other universities. At Oxford and Cambridge it is common form to enter for the Foreign Office examinations, and every facility is provided to acquaint students with the requirements and procedure, and encouragement is given by the faculty. More needs to be done in this regard at the other universities.

The intake is certainly more satisfactory, now that it is more diverse; but it is not possible to shake off the dust accumulated over years, and the lofty Victorian edifice which houses the Foreign Office retains an air of self-importance, if not superiority, which may affect even those with the least privileged background. New entrants are quickly assimilated and sometimes become more Foreign Office than those with long experience in the old tradition. There is probably no conscious effort to influence them but atmosphere is contagious. On the other hand, the absorption of the Consular Service has acted as a leaven and although it was formerly considered the inferior service, taking those who were not good enough for the Foreign or Diplomatic Service, it has been fully absorbed and former service with it in no way prejudices promotion. At least three senior Ambassadors entered by way of the Consular Service.

When reforms were being formulated it was realized that their full effect could not be felt for some time but that the transition could be assisted by provision for earlier retirement. This had long been desirable for the simple reason that not all members of the Service fulfil their early promise and some may reach the limit of their advancement before retiring age. Formerly, only harsh treatment was possible. The Secretary of State could dismiss such personnel outright or put them *en disponibilité*, in which case they remained in the Service but were not employed and were without pay. The Foreign Secretary can now compulsorily retire staff on pension without any discredit to them. There is provision for a hearing before an impartial board if desired. Some use has been made of this possibility of early retirement but there appears to be some resistance to its implementation. A similar camaraderie applies to some extent to appointments and promotions at the higher levels, and but for which Guy Burgess and Donald Maclean probably would have been dismissed the Service long before their flight beyond the Iron Curtain.

There is something wrong with a system which permits retention on responsible duties of those whose drunkenness and perversion are notorious as was that of Burgess and to a lesser extent that of Maclean also. In the lower grades officers are recommended by the head of the Personnel Department but higher posts both at home and abroad are considered by an appointments board, of which the Permanent Under-Secretary is chairman and which includes the Under-Secretaries, the Foreign Secretary's private secretary and one of the junior Ministers. Recommendations go through the Permanent Secretary to the Secretary of State who does not necessarily accept the board's recommendation.

A possible criticism of this latter method of promotion is that the appointments board is something of a closed shop and is not sufficiently influenced by outside objective judgment. Members of the board considered for any appointment do not appear, but obviously those who have the good fortune to be best known to its members have an unavoidable advantage over their lesser-known colleagues. The same may apply to the few who have come to the notice of the Secretary of State, by working for instance in the private office. One difficulty of promotion is that it must wait on retirement at the top, or promotion of immediate superiors, and the number of high-ranking posts abroad is limited. Whenever diplomatic relations are severed and ambassadors withdrawn there is one less post to fill, one more redundant diplomat, and an obstacle to promotion. When an ambassador is moved a general reshuffle ensues and ambassadors, ministers and counsellors are moved around as in a game of chess. For this among other reasons it is undesirable, save in very exceptional circumstances, to appoint outsiders as ambassadors. It is bad for the morale of the Service.

At the lower levels promotion is largely by seniority and ability and specialist knowledge does not appear to be taken always sufficiently into account; but in the long run merit counts, and since the reforms promotion for younger members showing ability has been greatly facilitated. A stimulus was given by the reforms to promotion within the service and from the junior to the senior branches. There are three channels for promotion to branch A. First, by special competition conducted by the Civil Service Commission for members of branch B and branch C nominated by the Foreign Office and between 25 and 30 years of age with a minimum of three years service; second, from branch B to grade 7 of branch A, selection being by a promotion board from those with 15-20 years experience; and third, for those in an even later stage of their career who on the recommendations of the promotion board can be transferred from branch B to grade 6 of branch A. There are also facilities for promotion on merit and seniority from branch C to the most junior grade of branch B.

Division between the respective branches is not as clear cut as might appear from the above. There is a certain amount of dove-tailing and some over-lapping. Branch A is the senior service as a branch and is concerned mainly with the conduct of foreign relations both at home and abroad while the other branches largely provide the necessary administrative and other ancillary services. Certain of the latter jobs, however, are more important than many of the former; others run parallel to each other and there is much intermingling. Many grades are common to more than one branch. In addition to the normal administrative grades of the Civil Service there are the diplomatic ranks which were first promulgated by the Congress of Vienna in order to end undignified disputes over precedence, which were then only too common. The consular section also has its own ranks. Each rank may cover a number of grades varying with seniority and the post. The 1955/6 estimates[1] for the diplomatic posts show that the officers employed in a representative capacity included 61 Ambassadors who had been drawn from grades 1 to 6; 17 Ministers Plenipotentiary from grades 3 to 6; 17 Ministers serving under Ambassadors from grades 3 and 5, 39 Counsellers from grades 5 and 6 and the 100 First Secretaries were in grade 7. Of 68 Consuls-General 17 were in grade 4, and 51 in grade 6.

The Foreign Office acts on the view that it is undesirable for anyone to serve too long in one post, it now being considered

[1] Civil Estimates. 1955/6. Class II p. 19.

desirable that all should have as wide and varied experience as is practicable. This is probably wise, but tours of duty of about three years, two in iron-curtain countries, are somewhat on the short side and the present tendency is to extend them. More encouragement is now given to specialization and greater account taken of it in making appointments. Further, the reforms have made it possible for a higher proportion of the staff to have periods of service in London, which is desirable to enable them not only to obtain a better knowledge of the working of the Foreign Office but also to become better acquainted with the way of life in the country they represent. This is essential and needs to be extended, as far too frequently in the past our representatives abroad have been deplorably out of touch with opinion at home. To assist in the latter, refresher courses are held for those on leave which include visits to industrial areas and special week-end courses in politics at Oxford.

Unlike the Foreign Service the Commonwealth Relations Service is part of the Home Civil Service. Entrance is by open competitive examination under both methods I and II with some preference for the latter, which is considered to provide for the better selection of the particular type of man required. The Service is of younger growth and derives from the former Dominions Office, which itself grew out of the Colonial Office. It joined forces with the India Office which for at least the last decade of its existence had been fully integrated into the Home Civil Service.

Like the Foreign Service since the reforms, it is a completely integrated service whose members usually alternate between service in London and overseas. Although its work is similar to that of the Foreign Office, with which it has close associations, it is better to regard it as running parallel to it. But its responsibilities and functions are distinct. It is the vehicle for consultation and communication between the members of the United Kingdom government and other Commonwealth countries. At home, it is responsible for advising ministers on policy *vis-à-vis* the rest of the Commonwealth, for assisting in the execution of government policy, for the co-ordination of the work of the various United Kingdom departments with other Commonwealth countries, for arranging consultations, and exchanging information with them. Overseas, it is responsible for staffing the British Embassy in Dublin and the United Kingdom High Commissioners' offices in Commonwealth countries, viz. Canada, Australia, New Zealand, South Africa, India, Pakistan, Ceylon, and the Federation of Rhodesia and Nyasaland. Its responsibility for relations with the Irish Republic results from the Ireland Act, 1949 under which the Irish Republic is not regarded as a foreign country although it is no longer a member of the Commonwealth; and accordingly the Secretary of State for Commonwealth Relations and not the Foreign Secretary became the Minister responsible for the United Kingdom's relations with it. There is no Consular Service as such, although in India and Pakistan there are Deputy High Commissioners' offices in different parts of the sub-continent and, following the changed nationality laws, passport offices have had to be created in major centres, and information offices are also organized outside the capitals. The far-reaching post-war constitutional developments within the Commonwealth which have been accompanied by the growing importance of the Commonwealth countries in international affairs (each of course being completely responsible for its own foreign policy and for maintaining its own relations with foreign countries) as well as other special requirements of inter-Commonwealth relations, has justified maintenance of this separate service. Consultation needs to be continuous and comprehensive, but special ties and common interests enables it to be less formal and tend to lead Commonwealth countries to work together in the international field.

The Commonwealth Service calls for few new entries annually since the United Kingdom based strength, including all grades from the Permanent Under-Secretary to part-time cleaners, totals only somewhat over 1,000, of whom less than half belong to the administrative grades, and about one quarter of whom would be serving abroad at any one time. In addition, there is approximately the same number of locally recruited staff, mainly clerical and subordinate, it obviously being possible to recruit locally within the Commonwealth to a greater extent than in foreign countries. In fact, in the Service, even at the higher levels, there is a considerable Commonwealth element in the main overseas posts.

The educational background of post-war entrants is similar

to that of the Foreign Service. Since 1946, the 73 recruits entering the grades of principal and assistant principal came from no
less than 65 schools, only one from Eton and none from Harrow,
the public school contributing the most being Cheltenham, which
sent three. Twenty-seven of the entrants went to Oxford, twenty-
three to Cambridge, and three to St. Andrews. Nine universities
contributed one apiece and eleven entrants had not attended a
university.

There is some temporary interchange between the Foreign
and Commonwealth Services. Some of the higher Commonwealth appointments have been filled by members of the Foreign
Service seconded for the purpose, and C.R.O. staff are also
seconded to British embassies abroad. For instance, at present
—1955—the Deputy High Commissioner in India comes from
the Foreign Service. A wider range of experience is gained, and
as the conditions of service are very similar no difficulty arises
on this score. All members of the Service are liable for service
at home or overseas and, in the case of Administrative Class
Officers, the latter amounts to about half their service. Specialization is encouraged to some extent but all are expected to obtain
as broad a knowledge as possible of the whole scope of political
and economic relations within the Commonwealth. There are
no specialist posts such as labour attachés in the Foreign Service,
and where specialists are required they are seconded from other
departments. Exceptionally, the conduct of overseas information
activities is generally in the hands of Information Class Officers.

The 1943 Foreign Service reforms were not made for their
own sake but to improve the efficiency of the Foreign Office.
Theoretically, at least, the Foreign Office does not make policy;
that is the responsibility of the Cabinet advised by the Secretary
of State. Once policy is laid down, the Service carries it out
through its representatives abroad. In practice however, it is in
a position to influence the Foreign Secretary, who is dependent
upon information received from the missions abroad, and upon
his advisers at home. All that reaches him flows through these
channels, and much may silt up *en route*. It is highly important,
therefore, that the heads of mission, who are finally responsible
for what is sent back home, and heads of department in the Foreign Office itself, are qualified to sift and assess all that reaches

71

them. Abroad, very frequently the circle of acquaintance of the embassy is too limited and too confined to a similar social set. Whether it is so depends upon the ambassador, and assisted as he is now with a staff drawn from a wider field, and with a larger range of attachés, including information officers and labour attachés (the latter in an inadequate number of posts), there is ample opportunity for the circle to be widened. Between them the embassy staff can have access to representative opinion and the difficulty is not so much in obtaining it but in assessing it and reducing it to manageable proportions for transmission to the Foreign Office. What finally is remitted depends largely upon the head of mission. At the worst his judgment may be at fault; he may have prejudices or be easily influenced by a small number of acquaintances; or on occasions he may be tempted to provide only the information that he thinks the office would prefer or that will please the Secretary of State. It is remarkable, for instance, that some embassies never come across adverse comments on the Secretary of State's speeches.

Abroad, the work of the Foreign Service is arranged on a regional basis with some differentiation of function within each region. Each mission covers four categories; diplomatic, commercial diplomatic, consular, and public information. The head of the mission is not only responsible for the traditional functions of the Diplomatic Service in regard to communication and negotiation with foreign governments but supervises the other branches of the Service. There is also a number of permanent delegations to international organizations such as the United Nations, Council of Europe, Coal and Steel Community etc., whose specialized functions are necessarily differently organized.

The Foreign Service is not helped by traditional standards of entertainment and the strict adherence to protocol expected of the diplomatic corps. But Tallyrand's dictum should not be overlooked: 'Seuls les sots se moquent de l'étiquette; elle simplifie la vie.' To lower the standard of entertainment unilaterally would be to lose prestige, but because the diplomatic corps of all countries lives and entertains at a level which is quite out of line with modern standards, a levelling down would be desirable, especially as too frequently its members tend to entertain other members of the corps rather than the people of the country to which they are posted. A reduction in entertainment could only be brought about by agreement between the respective countries. A more reasonable way of life would be welcomed by most of the Foreign Service to whom the weekly round of lunches, receptions and dinners is not only a social bore but a physical strain, and very hard on head and stomach alike. Less formality would lead to more valuable contacts and better health.

It is not only the level of entertainment that is out of line but also the general standard of living of those serving abroad which the generous system of overseas allowances makes possible. A recent report of the Select Committee of Estimates of the House of Commons[1] was highly critical of both entertainment and living standards and thus brought a reply from the Foreign Office[2] which, apart from drawing attention to a number of inaccuracies in the report, attempted to justify the present system. It made a plausible case, for it is clearly difficult to strike the right level to attract the most suitable and sufficiently diverse types to the Service and to enable them adequately to represent their country and uphold its prestige. At the same time it must avoid standards so disparate from those maintained at home that members of the Foreign Service cease to be truly representative of their home country. It is essential that allowances are high enough to enable requisite standards to be maintained without supplementation by private income otherwise one of the main purposes of the 1943 reforms would be defeated. For this reason the late Ernest Bevin instituted the present system of allowances which in some cases err on the side of generosity. But that is preferable to the reverse; and compensation must be provided for the inconveniences of service abroad, liability to frequent transfers, and family separation. The present allowances are based on a rather complicated system which provides rent, children's and marital allowances, car and clothes allowance, and certain privileges in regard to duty free goods all of which are designed to enable the requisite standard to be maintained abroad, and representation duties to be fulfilled adequately; and at the same time to make it possible for reasonable home com-

---

[1] Seventh report from the Select Committee of Estimates Session 1953/54.
[2] Comments on the Seventh Report from the Select Committee: Cmd. 9377.

mitments to be met. The proportion of salary which can then be retained at home frequently amounts to about one half of basic salary. Allowances are related to the local cost of living and any comparisons in sterling are meaningless. For instance, as the Foreign Office points out in its reply to the Select Committee, a typist in Moscow receiving the equivalent of £4000 p.a. is probably living no more comfortably than her colleague receiving £400 p.a. in London. Heads of missions receive a *frais* sufficient to permit upkeep of the official residence and provision of entertainment appropriate to the post; senior staffs receive entertainment allowances, expenditure of which does not have to be accounted for. The Select Committee suggested consideration of the refunding of actual expenditure on entertainment which is the more normal commercial practice, and the Foreign Office is to experiment with this at the lower grades—First Secretaries and below. This, however, carries certain disadvantages, and since business expenses are regarded as a supplementation of income and their designation on occasion is subject to somewhat flexible interpretation, it would be regrettable if this led to the introduction of similar business 'ethics' in the Foreign Service. The system of inspection exercises a check over expenditure abroad and of the level of overseas allowances. All foreign missions are visited periodically by the Foreign Service Inspectorate which consists of six senior officers with foreign experience who are responsible for checking on living conditions and making recommendations on establishment and allowances.

To deal intelligently with the vast quantity of material that is gathered in the restricted environment in which the diplomatic corps moves, it is essential that the staff stationed in London be of sufficient calibre and experience to bring its own judgment to bear on all incoming material and to relate it to the wider scene. To give the right weight to the man on the spot is highly important, and to know when to accept or reject his advice is difficult. That is the job of the departments of the Foreign Office. But some ambassadors can be consistently wrong and yet the office follows their advice, while others are persistently right and are ignored. How different would have been the course of foreign policy between the wars if the advice of Sir

Nevile Henderson when Ambassador to Germany had been rejected and that of Sir Eric Phipps and Sir Horace Rumbold accepted. On the whole, however, the Foreign Office is organized so as to be able to assess incoming information against a background of policy formulated over a long period. It is divided into political, functional and administrative departments. The nine political departments are responsible for the conduct of political relations with foreign powers in defined geographical areas and the twelve functional departments specialize in branches of activity irrespective of area. The nine administrative departments including finance, personnel, establishment, conferences and supply, are under the control of a Deputy Under-Secretary known as the Chief Clerk, while the other departments are grouped under Under-Secretaries.[1] Through them minutes will pass, and if advice is to be tendered to the Secretary of State or another Minister it will go to the Permanent Under-Secretary. His is in the last resort the policy department, but the Secretary of State decides both on immediate matters and those of longer term. Unfortunately, so hectic has been life in the Foreign Office, with complex problems falling over one another for immediate action, that long-term planning and policy formulation do not always receive adequate attention. Major policy is finally authorized for submission to the Foreign Secretary in the Permanent Under-Secretary's Department, and when there is time, which is far too infrequent, heads of departments may meet to discuss long-term policies in relation to major issues.

Often it is considered that the Foreign Office has too much power, exercises too great an influence on policy, and may even determine foreign policy. Of course it has considerable influence. No body of civil servants is in so favourable a position, because none has so much exclusive knowledge which is beyond the ability of its Minister to obtain. The Minister of a home department is obviously in an entirely different position. All weak Ministers can be led by their permanent officials but a strong Secretary of State need be no more pliable than any other Minister.

It is, however, extremely difficult to convey the extent to

[1] For full description of organization see *The Foreign Service* by Lord Strang. Ch. III.

which the Foreign Office is responsible for the formulation of policy. Undoubtedly the fact that its staff remains while Ministers come and go provides a continuity which gives its permanent Under-Secretary and his colleagues an advantage over the incoming Minister. The extent to which the Secretary of State will be influenced depends upon the strength of his personality and that of the Permanent Under-Secretary. The Foreign Secretary's may be a lone voice confronted by the solid united phalax of his permanent officials, and they can be as determined and as prejudiced in their views as any other intelligent and responsible body of persons. But the advice they tender will be based on policy already laid down; it will conform to the line previously accepted and in the long run it is only the Cabinet that can change that. Officers may well resist any suggested change and will use their persuasive powers on the Secretary of State but he is the person finally responsible for presenting foreign policy to the Cabinet. It is surprising how much goes to the Cabinet, where Foreign Office recommendations are by no means always accepted. The Foreign Office could not carry out policy contrary to that laid down by the Cabinet. It is no different from the Civil Service in loyally carrying out decisions even though they may be contrary to its judgment. But because of its experience and the continuity it represents some of the worst blunders of British foreign policy have been made when the least weight was given to the Foreign Office view, and the worst have frequently occurred when Prime Ministers have taken foreign policy unto themselves and out of the hands of their Secretaries of State. The period between the wars throws up some tragic examples of this and notably during the premiership of Neville Chamberlain, who was the worst offender of all. Not only did he reject the policy of the Foreign Secretary and follow a contrary line but he acted on occasions quite independently of him and brought in his own advisers from outside the Foreign Office, for instance Sir Horace Wilson who accompanied him to Munich.

It is equally difficult to assess the extent to which foreign policy is conditioned by the personalities manning the missions abroad. It is hard to say whether an ambassador influences policy or remains in his post because he reflects the viewpoint held by his government. This may well have been so with

Sir Nevile Henderson whose views and advice suited Chamberlain's appeasement policy. Undoubtedly ambassadors can still have considerable influence. It is a mistake to regard them as administrators merely carrying out instructions from London and acting as a two-way post office despatching information and receiving instructions. Considerable weight is given to their views, their advice is sought and the need for consultation and negotiation with foreign governments has by no means passed, for it cannot all be done in London. A head of mission with a strong personality expressing his views forcefully can have considerable influence on London within the limits of agreed policy. Equally his influence on the government to which he is accredited will depend on his personal relations with them. A trusted and personally-liked ambassador may achieve far more than one with greater ability but less popularity. Even in the post-war period, with communications bringing London and its missions so close, our relations with certain countries and the acceptance of desired policies have been greatly influenced for the better by the ability of the ambassador. The reverse is also true. It is impossible for a representative abroad to appreciate all the implications at the centre when he is on the periphery or for the man at home fully to anticipate the repercussions of policy determined at the Foreign Office on the periphery. A balance has to be struck between embassies abroad and the Foreign Office at home. The one should have an expert's knowledge gleaned on the spot, and the latter must be able to relate it to policy as a whole. There is an interplay and if a problem is of sufficient importance it will be resolved finally only after full consultation between the Secretary of State and the permanent officials concerned. It may be that only then are home politics taken into account.

The Foreign Office is strangely remote from Parliament and little conscious of the political repercussions of foreign policy on parliamentary opinion. It gets agitated about parliamentary questions but seems incapable of anticipating political reactions. Foreign affairs are never static and the world works to a 24-hour clock. The inflow of information and the demand for advice or instructions are never ceasing and the immediate and maybe lesser problem too frequently drives out the greater because it is less urgent. Matters that must be handled immediately are always jumping the queue and vital ones often remain until they too demand urgent solution and then there is no time to give them adequate thought. This is one of the major failings in the formulation of foreign policy. Inadequate provision for consideration of long term policy is probably the main fault of the present organization of the Foreign Office. The Permanent Under-Secretary is responsible to the Secretary of State, and, as stated, all submissions to Ministers filter through the Permanent Under-Secretary's department which can easily become a bottleneck. Rarely will recommendations go to any of the Foreign Office Ministers without passing across the Permanent Secretary's desk. As a consequence, although theoretically his department is responsible for policy, time is rarely available for consideration of other than immediate problems. Because there is no machinery for determining long term policy, and recommending its adjustment to current developments, decisions tend to be on an *ad hoc* basis. The nearest approach is the Permanent Under-Secretary's Committee, comprising the Deputy and Assistant Secretaries of State, which discusses major issues of policy. In practice, however, the pressure of immediate problems prevents its meeting regularly, and, valuable as such a committee could be, its deliberations are so infrequent, and its labours consequently spread over so long a period of time, that its contribution is quite inadequate to the need. It therefore appears desirable that responsibility for consideration of long term policy should be more definitely placed and the requisite machinery established. An under secretary without departmental duties might be given the responsibility for initiating consideration of policy in association and consultation with those concerned departmentally; and he might in the first instance report to a junior Minister. It is not suggested that the Foreign Office should be any more responsible for policy than at present but that machinery for its better consideration should be established so that there could be greater and more continuous deliberation on matters of policy and to which current problems can be better related. Harold Nicolson in one of the Chichele Lectures minds us of Richelieu's precept that diplomacy was not a mere *ad hoc* operation but a continuous process; that the art of negotiation must be a permanent activity and not merely a hurried endeavour; and that diplomacy should aim, not at incidental or opportunist arrangements, but at creating solid and durable relations.[1] Pressure on the Secretary of State and the senior staff is so great that adequate consideration cannot be given to matters brought to them for decisions or enough time found to weigh adequately the information that flows in ceaselessly. To delegate more to the junior Ministers as Mr Herbert Morrison advocates is difficult because it must stop short at final responsibility.[2] The Foreign Secretary's responsibility to the Cabinet cannot be shed. Further, one or more Ministers must spend much of the year at United Nations assemblies or other conferences. Consequently to increase the number of Ministers as the present Government has done to two Ministers of State and two Parliamentary Under Secretaries is not the answer. It may be found eventually in the appointment of a political deputy to the Foreign Secretary with delegated powers.

The difficulty remains that foreign affairs now concern so much that they overflow into defence, financial, economic and commercial fields. With the shrinking of the world as a result of the speed and nature of modern communications, the growth of internationalism generally and of international organizations in particular, and the political encroachment on international affairs, there is little into which foreign policy does not enter.

In these circumstances the importance of the Foreign Service increases and will continue to increase, so the calibre of its personnel must be maintained at the highest possible level, and the democratization of the Service speeded up. That is possible within the ambit of the 1943 reforms but more could be done to widen the field from which its personnel is drawn and to democratize the Services. No one can work with the Foreign Service without having a high regard for its integrity, intellectual ability, objective judgment and advice. The British Foreign Service deservedly ranks high among comparable services of other countries and it is gratifying at international conferences to find that Commonwealth delegations, and those of many other countries, turn to the United Kingdom representatives for guidance because it is so highly regarded and invariably the best served by its advisers and consequently the best briefed. All the same, improvement is possible both in regard to the formulation of

[1] *The Evolution of Diplomatic Method* by Harold Nicolson.
[2] *Government and Parliament* by Herbert Morrison. Ch. IV.

policy, recruitment and organization. More forward thinking is necessary. A central planning department would be out of keeping with the requirements of foreign policy, but an extension of the work of the Permanent Secretary's Committee in regard to the consideration of long-term policy would be advantageous. Policy problems should be the continuing responsibility of a specially assigned staff and not considered only when time permits. On the personnel side the main requirement is greater diversity of experience outside the Service which recruitment direct from school and university limits. Recruitment from an even wider field would assist and a greater entry from other universities than Oxford and Cambridge should be facilitated by the better acquainting of students of conditions of entry and facilitating preparation and entrance for the Foreign Service examination. Abroad there is need to put an end to the exclusiveness of the diplomatic corps, a reduction in the high standard of living and entertainment and some modification of protocol, much of which is an anachronism.

Chapter 7

THE COLONIAL SERVICE

By The RIGHT HON. A. CREECH JONES, M.P.
(Secretary of State for the Colonies, 1946-50)

THE Secretary of State for the Colonies recently announced
that as from 1st October 1954, the Colonial Service would be
constituted Her Majesty's Overseas Civil Service. The White
Paper issued by the Colonial Office revealed the anxieties felt in
the public services of the dependent territories, and the difficulties being experienced in London in the recruitment of young
men and women essential for these services. A Service which has
provided many remarkable men for the work of government in
the Colonies and Protectorates, and which has worked for decades with great devotion and efficiency, is in danger of founder-
ing because of the success of the policies it has encouraged
and helped to apply. For well over a century it has carried
exceptionally important responsibilities for the British Crown
and today there still remain vast territories where its work is
indispensable; but it is experiencing a crisis because of the conditions which have emerged in our contemporary world.

It was inevitable that the Service, such as it was in its early
days, should consist of men appointed from Britain or recruited
locally from the colonists. Later, members of the local population were more and more drawn into public work, but always
it was necessary to draw from Britain young men for service in
the administrative, professional and technical branches because
of the inadequacy or unsuitability of the local resources. But the
Colonial Service is a comparatively young Service, and from
time to time efforts have been made to systematize and regular-
ize it in relation to the whole field of public employment in the
dependencies overseas. Less than sixty years ago the Service
could not have been said to exist as a service in anything but
name. Twenty-five years ago the men and women brought into
the Service by the Colonial Office and recruited for the higher

81

branches, were constituted a unified service and organized into a number of unified branches. The institution of functional branches as unified services was intended to set a standard of qualification which would help to create efficient services in the colonies and secure a freer interchange of officers for the higher posts and provide a wider scope of promotion for the best officers. It was hoped thereby to improve the recruitment of specially qualified staff, and these would be liable for service in any territory, and could be transferred without promotion though not to a post of less value. Only British subjects or British protected persons were eligible for the Service.

It may be that the change somewhat confused the position of local entrants who might be eligible and engaged for jobs of marked responsibility, and who were permanent residents or native in the territories. All officers of the Colonial Services, unified or otherwise, are however regarded as servants of the the Crown and the Colonial Regulations lay down the conditions of their employment, the Secretary of State being the ultimate authority for appointments, promotions, discipline and general conditions. The double thread in the posts of the unified staff could not well be prevented. These men are under the general direction and patronage of the Secretary of State as well as in the direct employment of the Colonial Government. While they belong to a general service under the Crown and are eligible for service in other territories, they are also in the local Civil Service and are paid by the government they serve, which also shares in the provision for their ultimate superannuation. Though the public services of the colonies differ considerably from one another, each administration has its separate budget and the salaries of its civil servants are paid from local revenues whether or not those revenues are assisted from British funds.

Nearly all the principal posts in the colonies go to the men of the unified services and are consequently predominantly manned by men from Britain and the Commonwealth and directly appointed by the Secretary of State. These posts embrace the administrative, legal, agricultural, veterinary, education, medical, nursing, mines, forestry, engineering, chemical, postal, customs, prisons, police, civil aviation, survey, geological survey, audit and research branches of the Colonial Service, each branch being a unified service with its own regulations. They provide the framework of all government activities, and on them depend the order, welfare and development of the territory and its people. The smooth working and efficiency of these branches are vital factors in the progress to self-government, and are just as vital subsequently.

Few colonies are yet able to supply their own fully trained Civil Service. Most of the men in the ranks of the public services are of local origin but the practice is to supplement them in the higher grades by officers recruited from the United Kingdom or transferred from other colonies. Even in the case of the West Indies, some of the highest posts are occupied by members of the unified colonial service. In the case of Southern Rhodesia, formerly a self-governing colony, the government, which is European, engage their own service. Elsewhere, in British Africa the process of providing local personnel for the higher reaches has not gone far. While a substantial part of the work in all government offices is done inevitably by members of the local population, the main direction and organization of administration of the technical and professional services is largely in the hands of expatriate members of the unified services and not of local people.

'Africanization' has indeed proceeded at a very slow pace because of the alleged absence of competent and suitable candidates and the prejudice of the official hierarchy. The nationalist spirit has now outpaced all that governors could forsee a few years ago, or were disposed to provide for. In the Gold Coast and Nigeria the process of staffing the administration with Africans is being rapidly accelerated, but for a long time to come the inexperience, immaturity, inadequacy and small number of skilled Africans will be an effective obstacle to the attainment of an indigenous service, however desirable and necessary that is in those African countries which have been inspired in recent years by a new political awareness.

As it is, no less than 12,000 first appointments of all kinds, in all the colonies, have been made by the Colonial Office alone since the war ended, an average rate of intake five times that of the years just before the war. Appointments to the higher grades were 1,227 in 1953 and 1,378 in 1952, but the number of unfilled vacancies was still about a thousand. These figures of recruitment illustrate not only the dependence of the territories on the flow of candidates from Britain, but also the shortcomings of earlier policies. Because administrations are anxious to maintain a high standard of work and not lower the qualifications for admission to their services they are experiencing a shortage of officers and rejecting less qualified local persons. This means a great strain on existing officials who are not only short-handed, but already have additional burdens to carry. They have little time to train the local recruits who may be available, but who in any case, in spite of their inexperience, are in desperate demand. The progress to self-government with the dwindling number of unified officers and unfilled vacancies is thus creating misgivings in the unified colonial services. At least, some of their members are feeling doubt as to how thoroughly they should work for their own displacement or how much they should lend themselves to a process which may end their career.

This malaise in the Colonial Service is a striking feature in any consideration of the problems facing the Service. The disruption of careers by the termination of British authority in a territory is not a new feature in the history of British overseas administration, although the dissolution of British authority in India, Pakistan, Burma, Jordan, Ceylon and Palestine has in a brief period of years thrown up the problem in alarming relief. The recent rapid events in the Sudan and West Africa have added to the apprehensions of the Service. The consequences of the granting of autonomy and independence have been generously met by the local governments in terms of compensation and pension provision to the staffs concerned, and the transition period has been eased to avoid personal hardship or to meet the needs of the service after the change of authority. Though careers under one government have come to an end, in many cases they have been no more than interrupted (distasteful as that may be). Transfer to the service of another territory has been offered by the Colonial Office. Nonetheless, the possibility of redundancy or interruption of service does not encourage members of a Service to equip themselves better for their work, or to acquire qualifications, such as native languages, intimate anthropological knowledge, native law and practice, and other social and economic matters associated with the life of the communities they serve. In the past, much distinction has been enjoyed by the Service because of this contribution to knowledge—language, natural science, anthropology, etc.—and to the greater efficiency of government. A Service which has worked hard for political development as an act of trust and British faith, now sees the pace to self-government and independence accelerating everywhere, and that pace no less fast outside Africa (where most of the dependent Commonwealth is), in the countries of S. E. Asia and the Caribbean. They see also, with the increasing devolution of authority from London to the colonies, and the closing-in of prospects in all directions, the British Government no longer able to exercise effective control over their tenure and conditions of employment as hitherto.

Yet while this process to self-government is advancing, the range of functions of government increases and more officials are wanted, as well as greater experience and expertise. In all the British territories programmes of economic and social development are in progress. All demand to be equipped with the usual public works, utilities and services of the modern state and to open out their natural resources for higher standards of living. There is consequently an increasing demand in the colonies for highly skilled officials and staff and a widening opportunity for men with experience who are capable of handling the complex and constantly expanding administration of the territories. These opportunities and prospects are not contracting provided that men and women will agree to serve as advisers and guides to governments of different colour, and provided such governments will guarantee suitable conditions and satisfactory contracts.

As we have noted, a large number of the existing vacancies are not being filled from Britain, while at the same time many men are leaving the Service because of their dwindling prospects, their feeling of insecurity, or their lack of confidence in their new government. With the ferment of nationalism in the territories, the rapid increase in political responsibility of the local governments, and the inadequate educational facilities, insufficient time remains for the complete transformation of the administrative, technical and professional services into native services, that are sufficiently trained and experienced for the duties to be performed.

The situation has been recognized by the responsible leaders in most territories, including the Gold Coast and Nigeria, where self-government is near realization. The offer of guarantees and the giving of assurances, the making of short or long term contracts of service, the attempt to reconcile the remuneration of expatriates with local staff, of Africans with non-Africans, have preoccupied the responsible leaders in many territories. But the loss of experienced staff to private enterprise goes on, as it does to other colonial governments and to less exacting livelihoods. A severe toll has been laid on the Colonial Service in spite of the sincere efforts of native leaders and governments to stop the leak which is threatening the progress of the territories on the eve of their 'liberation'.

So far as one can ascertain, that loss has been accentuated to a less extent than might have been expected by an indisposition of men of the unified services to work under a 'foreign' government, or by a dislike of filling advisory positions and acting under the direction of native Ministers exercising responsibility. All the evidence points to the full co-operation and disinterested service offered by the men whose authority is now diminished. But such a situation calls for restraint and patience both on the side of the new men in whom authority now reposes, and on the side of the men in the expatriate service whose lives are now more precarious and complicated. Other adjustments must also occur in the local services which formerly existed to serve the purposes of an 'alien' government, for with the arrival of a native democratically responsible government, changes must be made in the tone and structure of administration. The situation is perhaps more ambiguous in regions where territories have become grouped, as in the case of the Central African Federation. There, the responsibility of officials and the differences in conception of policy may sometimes give rise to suspicion regarding fundamental loyalties, because of the traditional policy of the Colonial Office on the one hand, and the views of the predominantly white settler government of the Federation on the other.

I have tried to set out some of the factors which are causing anxiety to the expatriate members of the Colonial Service and which in recent years have hampered the enlistment of men for the unified services from Britain. The technical services have suffered as well as the administrative. Men with technical qualifications and professional skill have found their services in demand at satisfactory pay and conditions in less adventurous services at home or in the international field. Although improvements in pay and conditions have been made in the colonies, (and adjustments have often produced complicated reactions between the various services), the services have lagged behind and have not been made sufficiently attractive. In a world in which rehabilitation and development are urgent and offer attractive opportunities, in which great social and economic changes are taking place and in which international organization is playing an increasing part, the limited resources and economic difficulties in the colonies have reacted against the opportunities and conditions of employment of the men whose skills are most sought after. The work in some of the colonies has been augmented by technicians under schemes of international or American aid, or by the secondment of men and women from British public services (teaching, medical, prisons, etc.), with guarantees against loss of increments and seniority as a result of their absence from Britain on period contracts. But young cadets from the universities of Britain have had reasonable doubts whether their life career should be made in colonies which are finding internal influences and external pressures to self-government irresistible.

Her Majesty's Overseas Civil Service has consequently been instituted in the place of what was formerly known as the Colonial Service and new regulations defining the conditions and eligibility for admission to it and the rights and obligations of its members have been made. The British Government propose to observe the necessary safeguards provided by the former Colonial Regulations or the constitutional instruments of any territory under their responsibility, and will enter into formal agreement with the government of a territory if, and when, it attains self-government for the observance of the conditions of the appointments. So long as the servants of that government remain in their existing employment, the government concerned will not alter their terms of service so as to make them less favourable than those on which the officers are already serving. Their pension rights and other benefits will be safeguarded. The officers will be regarded as members of H.M. Overseas Service and be eligible for consideration for transfer or promotion to any posts which the Secretary of State may be requested to fill in other territories, and the local government will not unreasonably withhold its consent. Adequate notice will be given of any intention to terminate employment in consequence of constitutional changes, and compensation will be paid by the local government in the event of premature retirement as a result of such changes. The British Government will endeavour to find alternative employment should the officer so desire.

In respect of future vacancies in territories attaining self-government, and in the filling of which the British Government is asked to co-operate, the appointments will be arranged between the British and employing governments and a clear statement made whether the post carries with it membership of the Overseas Civil Service or merely a contractual relationship with the territorial government. Both types of employment would involve the officer as being in all respects responsible to the territorial government.

By such arrangements, the British Government hopes to restore the confidence and sense of security of the members of the Colonial Service and to ensure that qualified men and women may be attracted to come forward in future as in the past 'in a spirit of confidence, enthusiasm and partnership to help the overseas governments and peoples along the path of social, economic and political progress'.

Whether these assurances and safeguards will allay the existing doubts and anxieties remains to be seen, but the colonial governments are pressing on so far as their own local services are concerned, with the expansion of facilities for higher education both in the territories and by scholarships to the British universities and institutes of learning, are introducing more and more native peoples into the services with less exacting standards of qualification than previously obtained (a policy which in earlier days was resisted by British officials at home and in the colonies), and are seeking an answer to the discontent which arises among native officers whose income is below that paid to persons brought in from Britain. In some territories where no popular opprobrium attends certain practices which prejudice the integrity and esteem of the service, there are difficulties in building up a disinterested service, actuated by a deep sense of public responsibility and service; there is a real danger that efficiency and integrity in the services will suffer.

It is with all these difficulties in mind that the work of the Colonial Service should be assessed. Its virtues are considerable. Much can be criticized regarding its enlistment and structure, the defects of its conventions and organization, but the massiveness of its contribution and achievement, its sense of responsibility and service to the colonial people, its quality of fair play, tolerance, and patience, are worthy of record. Much of its work is done in exhausting conditions which are not helpful to morale. It is work which provokes anxiety, and involves solitude, danger, and the lassitude of diminished health. It carries considerable and often over-burdening responsibility. It has frequently been a shield of the people against abuses and unjust intervention from whatever quarter. It has sought to guide and persuade rather than to impose the will of government. In places, unhappily, it has sometimes nodded, and lapsed from its high standards, and on occasion a few of its highest officers have been deaf or blind to legitimate aspirations and public needs. A complacency has sometimes afflicted its initiative and energy. But when all is said and done, it has performed a great benevolent work, and thrown up great administrators and social pioneers; it has extended the frontiers of civilization and helped towards the unification of the world. Whatever one may dislike or reject in 'colonization', the great dedication of many of the members of the Colonial Service and the devotion and service rendered deserve our mead of recognition in this present phase when the old habits of imperialism are surrendering to new conceptions of freedom and world order.

It is necessary to make clear that members of the Colonial Service do not staff the Colonial Office. The officers of that Office form part of the Home Civil Service. They have opportunities of visiting the colonies and for periods up to two years of serving in the Colonial Service. Six such officers were posted in 1952 and seven in 1953. There is a reciprocal movement of the Colonial Service into the Colonial Office, and this brings a refreshing stream of direct colonial experiences into the life of that Office. Six colonial officers took up duty in the department in 1952, and six in 1953. The arrangement could be extended with mutual advantage. Since 1945, the Colonial Office, too, has been greatly expanded to allow for the changing and developing responsibilities of the Secretary of State, and has transformed

its character. The constructive effort towards colonial development and welfare has brought the Office in wider and more
active contact with colonial affairs. New departments of the
Office have been created concerned, for instance, with economic
development and commerce and trade, with mining and industrial development, with surveys and educational advance, with
colonial finance and social services, with research and local
government, and with publicity and international relations. It
offers help and service, technical and financial aid; it conducts
investigations and performs a thousand odd services to assist
colonies to advance; besides, it continues to perform what is left
of the traditional duties of supervising and directing the administration and legislation of the territories for which the Secretary
of State is responsible. The organization of the Office is not
simple when problems have to be dealt with as matters of policy
for the dependencies of the Commonwealth as a whole, and also
studied in their geographical setting as part of the policy, and
related to the problems, of a single territory. The Colonial
Office also watches the interest of the Colonial Service, fills its
vacancies and highest posts, recruits and trains the cadets in the
unified services and offers broad lines of direction and policy to
guide governors and their staffs.

The Colonial Service is mainly recruited from the universities
of Oxford and Cambridge and London. The new universities in
the provinces, for a variety of reasons, provide only a very small
proportion of the candidates, a fact that is regrettable in view
of the variety of needs in the territories. The number of candidates from the countries of the Commonwealth, in spite of the
special machinery of selection in their universities, is negli-
gible. There is no competitive examination for appointments, but
a good academic qualification is called for, and selection is made
by an interviewing Board, made up of men and women of varied
experience in public life at home and overseas. The age limit is
28, and I hope candidates of wider than school experience are
still given advantage in assessment, other things being equal.
Because of the complex nature of the work in the territories
it is desirable that the qualification of recruits should be on
a wide basis. The growing life in the territories undoubtedly
needs in the higher places of political and technical administration men of great intelligence, perception and sympathy;

but it also needs an ingredient of experience in the active affairs of the modern world. After the war, men were recruited from the forces, as well as from the universities. In addition, recruitment was at a higher age than normally and men of good educational qualification were invited to apply who had some experience of finance and industry, of local government and social affairs, and knowledge of other walks of life than in a centre of higher learning. The Selection Board also tries to discover the attitude of candidates to race and colour discrimination, and would eliminate men with deep prejudices regarding such matters. But the number of recruits of the right standard falls short of the requirements in the territories.

A period of training follows on selection and assignment to the vacancies to be filled. Since 1924 training courses for most branches of the Service have been established. The courses of training have received the most careful thought of the Colonial Ministers and their advisers, and it is not too early to say that the expense of this special training has been fully justified. The older universities and London have played an important part in devising the courses and making facilities for the studies required. The first course for administrative officers is a year; for the technical and professional men it is longer. The subjects include a native language, native law and custom, as well as a rapid survey of political and social institutions (e.g. local government, trade unionism, co-operation) and economics. After their first tour of 15 to 18 months in the territory to which they are appointed (in some instances after the second tour), cadets return for a further course of training at one or other university so that in the light of the experience they have gained their further studies may be related to the practical background of their territory. The experiment in training has been flexible and adapted to needs and experience. Cadets from the colonies study alongside cadets selected in Britain, and in the clubs established in Oxford, Cambridge, and London a good camaraderie is created among all taking the first and second courses. The wives of the men are also encouraged to interest themselves in the problems facing their husbands and may participate in the studies. This feature is important because of the special contribution which women can make in colonial life.

I laid it down in 1946 that it must be regarded as an accepted principle in appointments to the Colonial Service that there should be no barriers to colonial candidates or colonially recruited public servants for any post which they are qualified to fill. Salaries of the Colonial Service should be determined according to the nature of the work and relative responsibilities irrespective of the race or domicile of the individuals occupying the posts; the rates should be applicable to locally recruited staff and expatriation allowances should be paid to officers employed from Britain and their passages assisted on their taking leave. Poor colonies should not be at a disadvantage in obtaining the services of fully qualified staff and if necessary should seek financial aid from the United Kingdom. Public Service Commissions should deal with Service matters and be responsible for the selection and appointments of local candidates to local service posts. These principles have become generally applicable since.

It is of interest to mention that it is intended to make in the career of the colonial servant a feature of the sabbatical year, after seven years service or more. Such a year would provide the occasion for refreshment of mind and revision of study in the light of experience gained. It would afford opportunity of study of some special subject which the officer is concerned with, or it might offer the prospect of a visit to the administration of another colonial power for comparative study. As it is, colonial officers on leave have special facilities for summer schools or week-end conferences in England arranged to study special colonial problems or phases of modern political and social policy. Some of these conferences in which a wide range of experience has been pooled and systematized have been of great value to the Secretary of State in giving a lead to colonial governments in respect to a new phase of policy. There are now periodical conferences of officers of particular services drawn from all the territories or organized on a regional basis. In addition, a 'house' journal of the Service circulates in all the colonies for the purpose of strengthening the *esprit de corps* of the service and informing officers on policy, parliamentary discussion and experiments. The immense importance of breaking down the isolation which many colonial service men and women experience in their work cannot be over-emphasized. They should feel that they are in contact with the life of their service and territory, that they are not kept in ignorance of policy whether made in their territory or London, that they know of experiments being made in other territories and by other colonial powers, and that they are conscious of the influences at work in the contemporary world. They should have opportunities of consultation and meeting fellow officers in conference and of refreshing their minds after the exacting life in the hinterland of the territory they serve. Much is being done in this direction, but governors should appreciate still more the value and importance of such facilities to their staff.

Cadets usually enter on their early tours in the colony to which they are appointed with great hopes and enthusiasm. Some find themselves performing arduous duties of responsibility in the bush or at some isolated station; others work too close to District Officers or Resident Commissioners who may have lost their enthusiasm in the routine and unrewarding work they do. Too many find it difficult to make the intimate contact with the people in the villages because of the increasing quantities of paper work and new functions which fall to government. Their pay is often felt to be inadequate for the circumstances of the life and the new home responsibilities of children and their education in Britain that are incurred. Too often they are denied residence at a particular station for long and move from house to house after each leave. But as seniority advances and the 'dead wood' is removed from the Service (a fact now possible with the concession of early retirement age), the young officers supervise large areas of administration, control expenditure, co-operate with the technical services, watch the operations of the native courts and promote the welfare of the people of their areas. Government may be by indirect or by direct rule, but in any case, it calls for a degree of supervision and advice to the people's representatives so that the objects of government are promoted. The extension of genuine local government in the place of indirect rule should in time lessen at least some of the responsibility of the District Officers or Resident Commissioners although their aid and advice may be more necessary as central government hands some of its authority to the locality and regions. And, of course, there is an alteration in the title of their post.

It should be added that there are limitations imposed on

colonial civil servants respecting ownership of land in the territory they serve, respecting engagement in business and agriculture, and respecting participation in political associations (an increasing difficulty where native people enter the public services and who may be the most educated section of the community). These rules are salutary. Administrative officers are also urged to move about their districts as much as circumstances will permit and are indeed, in some territories, required to become proficient in a local language before they are confirmed in their appointments. They may also be required to pass further tests before they can pass certain points in their salary scales. Bonuses may be paid for additional languages.

As to offers of transfer for service in another territory, junior officers feel that the knowledge and experience they gain should be utilized as far as possible in the territory to which they are assigned. Transfers should not occur except for special reasons and not before a reasonable time has been completed in a particular post. On the other hand, the official excuse for transfers is that while they occasionally lead to some lack of continuity in service, with results that militate against efficiency, this fact is far outweighed by the wider experience which the policy of interchangeability enables officers to bring to their subsequent tasks. But too frequently the public interest is sacrificed when men of experience and qualification are transferred from districts they know and where they are known by the people, to districts where they have to become familiar with the language, the people and their customs.

The pinnacle of the Colonial Service in each territory is the governor. Governors are classified, and prestige, responsibility and authority differ considerably among them. There are five groups and according to some arbitrary decision as to the importance of a territory, so it is classified. The salary and allowances attached to these appointments vary accordingly. Consequently governors are not necessarily appointed to posts where their experience and qualifications are most needed, but according to their seniority, and the pay of the post. The result is bad. It is unsound that territories should have posted to them only the governors they can afford to pay. A poor colony in desperate need with very limited resources often cannot have the first-class men that are available and which it sorely needs.

Constitutional objections may be made to giving some financial assistance to colonies to enable them to get the best officials they need for coping with their problems. But the old-fashioned system of grading colonies is outmoded, and in its place a system of subvention in respect of certain high offices might be adopted by the British Government. Indeed, it may be a line of advance to constitute a special wing of the Service, directly employed and paid for by the United Kingdom, and made up of governors and other high functionaries such as colonial secretaries and the principal finance administrators. Their loyalty would, of course, be to the territorial government they served, but such an arrangement would offer a wider opportunity of selection for the work which the respective colonies require to be done. The creation of a Commonwealth or a Colonial Service employed and financed by the British Treasury offers undoubtedly complicated administrative and constitutional as well as financial problems, but an inquiry into the difficulties is overdue.

The influence and authority of governors are still considerable and important. Where political progress is advanced in a territory, their powers, though diminished, are great indeed. It is important that they should be good administrators and sympathetic to the aspirations of the people in their territory. But often their experience has been limited to colonial life among people of small social and political experience, in territories where the approach to governmental problems is altogether different from places where people are more mature and advanced in social experience. With the great surge of nationalistic and racial consciousness and the demand of the people for more responsibility and experience in the working of political institutions, it is evident that governors should bring a deeper and wider experience to bear on the problems which are urgent and important in their territories. The conditions of the world have changed in the past decade or so and the Colonial Service should recognize the importance, in some of the appointments that have to be made, of securing governors who can bring political knowledge and experience to the task of handling some of the difficult and complex matters which are emerging in the political development of certain of the colonies. Moreover, the Secretary of State relies on information supplied by his officials and particularly the governors. He sometimes is obliged to accept the advice of the representative on the spot, but while such advice may be objective, he cannot check views which may unconsciously be affected by local pressures and influences of all kinds. The integrity and informed judgment of governors is therefore of great importance and great care should be taken that the right man should be appointed.

All branches of the Colonial Service should be able to offer their best men for consideration for the post of governor. Governors have on occasion been taken from other branches than the administrative source, and some of them have done distinguished work. Some governors have come from the Colonial Office itself. It is taken for granted that in the case of certain territories (e.g. Gibraltar), someone who has attained high rank in the forces should be appointed but even here merely military appointments will no longer do. The attempt should be made always to get the best possible men from whatever source who are able to measure up to the job. It is not good that governorships should be regarded as the 'plums' of the Colonial Service.

A bad practice has established itself whereby governors and high civil servants often accumulate their leave and enjoy it towards the end of their service. It not infrequently happens that a governor is many months absent from his territory before the arrival of the new governor. The place of the governor is taken by the local colonial secretary during the long period of the governor's absence, and sometimes that secretary is inexperienced and inadequate for the duties which have to be performed. Instances have occurred of grave crises arising in such periods of absence, and the result is that the colony has appeared to lack leadership and direction. Such a situation in a colony involving difficulty by the absence of the governor ought to be avoided and governors and others should be required to take their leave as it becomes due. The period before the arrival of the new governor ought to be shortened.

A number of suggestions have been made in public discussion for improving the effectiveness of the Colonial Service and promoting its greater efficiency. The establishment of joint Councils for considering pay and conditions and the setting up of Public Commissions for dealing with the public services, their appointments and promotions, have served desirable purposes. As it is, to secure promotion men have sometimes to be transferred to another territory where their experience is wasted, and knowledge of language useless. To meet this difficulty the proposal has been made that the Service should be organized on regional lines so that officers would not be required to move from the region in which they were originally enlisted and in which their valuable experience has been gained. Other steps have been suggested. The practice of secondment from the Home Civil Service might be extended and also the practise of short or long term contracts for teachers, doctors and other callings without prejudice to their subsequent position in the profession at home.

But a more fundamental change has also been urged and it involves complicated constitutional issues. Just as the Colonial Development and Welfare Act of 1940 marked a new conception of the responsibilities of Britain and of the relationship of the United Kingdom and the colonies, so the political, economic and social changes in the colonies now compel a new conception of the administrative and technical aid which might be given by Britain. A new way needs to be found of assisting the territories in staffing their highest posts. There might be created a new and unified service which would guarantee security and reasonable prospects for its members and offer all the territories for their highest posts the most suitable men available. The British Government should underwrite the pay, continuity of employment and pension rights, and contribute to the cost of the Service. It might be recruited not only in Britain but also from the dependent and independent countries of the Commonwealth, and be financed as a development cost by the British Treasury. These men would obviously be regarded as in the employment of the government of the territory they are serving for the time being, and the governor would still act as the representative of the Crown and remain in his present relation with the Secretary of State. There would need to be safeguards against too great mobility for such men though obviously there would sometimes be advantage in having experienced men who could discharge special pieces of work for comparatively short periods to help a colony with a special or temporary difficulty. The time has come when the suggestion should be probed and the best use made of the remarkable body of men who have served the British and colonial public so well.

Chapter 8

THE STRUCTURE OF THE CIVIL SERVICE

By H. R. G. GREAVES

(Reader in Public Administration in the University of London)

I

EXTENSION of state activity in the twentieth century has wrought big changes in the general picture of the Civil Service. The more obvious of these are three: an immense increase in size; the inclusion within it of a large body of professional, scientific and technical staff, now actually outnumbering the administrative and executive officials, yet fitting uneasily into its hierarchical structure; and the spreading outwards from Whitehall of important fields of its work with a consequent geographical dispersal of its emplacement.

In the middle of 1955—and speaking in thousands—there were 248 civil servants in the Post Office and 388 in all other departments. Analysis of the latter according to the functions of their offices is highly instructive, for it reveals how small a part of the whole is now taken up by what may be regarded as the older functions of government, those classified as 'central government, home and legal departments' and 'foreign and imperial services'; these together amount to 32, or less than the staff of a single social service department, the Ministry of Pensions and National Insurance. The revenue departments have another 67. Those classified as dealing with 'trade, industry and transport' have 69, while offices concerned with the social services have 65. And the remainder of the staff in civil establishments are the 21 who are mainly in the Ministry of Works, the Ordnance Survey and the Stationery Office, denominated 'agency services'. This makes a total of 254, which compares with 134 in the defence departments—Admiralty, War, Air, and Supply—ranging from 27 to 39 each.

It is significant too that by far the largest of the civil departments are those in which there is the maximum dispersal. Again omitting the Post Office, although this partly revenue department is perhaps the most obvious case, these are the Inland Revenue itself, with 52, and the Ministries of National Insurance and Labour, with respectively 37 and 23. These, taken with the Post Office and the defence departments, whose staff is similarly scattered, bring the total in such offices of dispersed staffs to almost half a million, or ten-thirteenths of the total of civil servants.

Analysis of the Civil Service according to the classes into which it is divided shows that the number in the administrative or policy-making grade has rather more than doubled since shortly before the war. The executive, clerical and specialist grades have grown proportionately even more, perhaps the most striking increase being in the last group. The figures as they were in July 1955 are to be seen in the following table[1]:

	Established & Permanent Unestablished	Unestablished	Total
1. Administrative (Home)	2,596	165	2,761
2. Administrative (Foreign)	707	7	714
3. General Executive	35,493	1,581	37,074
4. Departmental Executive	28,432	1,977	30,409
5. General Clerical	79,200	11,709	90,909
6. Departmental Clerical	30,265	1,290	31,555
7. Clerical Assistants and Temporary Clerks III	35,609	27,554	63,163
8. Typing	16,475	11,061	27,536
9. Inspectorate	2,467	426	2,893
10. Messengers, Porters, etc.	21,264	16,308	37,572
11. Post Office Manipulatives	166,625	32,900	199,525
12. Professional, Scientific and Technical I	17,166	5,174	22,340
13. Scientific and Technical II	32,357	17,357	49,714
14. Ancillary Technical	26,163	13,108	39,271
Totals	494,819	140,617	635,436

There is thus defined the established hierarchy of the Civil Service with its levels determined by education and age at entry. Its principles are still those of the Northcote-Trevelyan report although the simple distinction between intellectual and mechanical kinds of work made therein has now been given a much more complex and gradual application. Also the idea of unification, that is of a single service, put forward in that report, while it

[1] From the 'Digest of Civil Service Staff Statistics', 1955.

underlies the extended development of classes common to the whole Service, has not proved susceptible of universal application, considerable departmental classes and special groups remaining as exceptions to it. And finally, as this table bears striking testimony, the specialist elements coming at the end of the hierarchy, groups 12-14 in the table, fall outside its ordinary structure forming a separate pyramid of their own.

This principle of hierarchy, so fundamental to the structure of the Service, has always been subjected to criticism and might well be re-examined today. But its most significant feature, recruitment of those destined to fill the principal posts, those concerned with management and the making of policy, from university graduates has well maintained its force. We need for such work minds which have been given the best education the nation provides. From the outset of reform, however, a competing principle was also strongly urged, namely 'the opening to officers of the lowest rank the opportunity for eventual advancement to the highest offices in the Service', as it was put by a head of the Department of Customs who was a contemporary of Trevelyan and who attributed the superior efficiency of that office to the adoption of this practice. The argument, it is true, was ably turned by the latter with the reply: 'In other words a system has been introduced into the Department of Customs very similar, so far as the regulation of promotion is concerned, to that which we propose for the whole public service.' But this was in fact to overlook, or rather to fail to foresee, the effectiveness of the barriers to promotion constituted by the grade divisions. It was to prove extremely rare for these ever to be surmounted and the obstacle they established was to become a standing grievance to the lower grades. Critics have also rightly laid stress on the social effects of this hierarchical structure, for inasmuch as university education was the privilege of the wealthy the administrative grade must be recruited mainly from a narrow social class out of touch with the general population.

More recent developments, however, and especially those of the last decade, have done something to remove the grounds for these strictures. It is also relevant that, since the Tomlin Commission in 1931 drew the distinction, and in practice earlier, it has been recognized that while some departments concerned mainly with policy require only or chiefly administrative and

clerical officers, others concerned mainly with applying a code of
law require chiefly executive and clerical officers, examples of the
latter being offices whose principal work is dealing with taxation
or insurance. For this has helped to diminish the sense of frustration of the executive class *vis-à-vis* the administrative, and to
assimilate clerical and executive.

Apart from this there have been four changes, one of which
may possibly be transitory. This is the rapidly expanded intake,
which applied to higher as well as lower staff, to meet the vastly
extended work of government for war and post-war development. This meant much new blood at the higher levels drawn
either directly from the outside fields of business, professional or
academic life or from elements within the public service but not
originally in the administrative class. While these were at first
temporary many remained on the establishment. Secondly, and a
more permanent source of change, is the great strides made towards equalizing educational opportunity in the country as a
whole. The effect of making university education increasingly the
reward of merit rather than of birth must be to widen the social
basis of administrative class recruitment although it has not as
yet done so as much as some have claimed. Thirdly, the growth
of attention to post-entry training and the newly recognized
responsibility of the Treasury for dealing with this has made a
promising beginning in what might well become an important
means of reducing hierarchical rigidities. More will be said
about this below. Finally, it must not be forgotten that, despite
their present weakness as a group within the hierarchy, the very
considerable growth in the numbers and significance of the professional and scientific officers in the Service, placing them near
to the sources of administrative decision and in close contact
with the highest administrators, has given them opportunities of
scaling the heights of which some at least have been able to
avail themselves.

But, as has been said, these 'specialists' create a further problem. It is in fact a twofold one. There is first the question of their
place in the hierarchy, that is of the relative status and pay
accorded them. Some support was given by the Chorley Committee to their dissatisfaction with the actual position, and there
can be little doubt that they have suffered in the past from a tendency among the more conservative elements at the administra-

tive level to disparage the technologist. Many of the top professional posts, however, are now at Deputy-Secretary level, and some even higher, although never as high as the administrative head of a department. Second is the question of function. Here their case though often more passionately put forward is really weaker. It is repeated in paragraph 87 of their latest Royal Commission evidence where they claim that the principal professional officers 'must be in a direct line of responsibility to the Minister and there should not be any interpolation of another officer purporting to hold responsibility and to give advice when in fact he can become only a transmitter of the advice of others. Transmission of professional advice is full of danger when it is done by a non-professional person. It is also, and this is the primary point, a means of lowering the value and status of the professional person and thereby demeaning the whole profession and structure.' There can certainly be no doubt that there should always be direct access to the Minister when either side wishes it but there is no suggestion that this is not the actual practice. The case really rests, however, on a mistaken view of the functions of the permanent and political heads of a department. Those of the former are to be the general manager of his department. Though subject, of course, like every other official, to the decision of the Minister it is his duty to run the department, to canalize all its activities, to have ready at any and every moment a recommendation on any and every issue of policy. The final decision, it is true, is the Minister's but so is his decision how and when to intervene in the affairs of the department, it being his business to 'see that it is run' in accordance with the policy of the government as a whole of which he is a member with responsibilities wider than those of his department. This position is properly met by the departmental structure which the specialists criticize; it would not be by what they advocate. Nor does the fact that in some departments the permanent headship is in some measure put into commission in the form of a council or board in any way affect the validity of these principles.

Finally, since the key to many of these aspects of the discussion lies in the character of the administrative class as the apex of the Service, it must be pointed out that today less than in the past is that body a segregated caste relatively to the rest of the Service. In 1950 rather more of its established members had come into it by way of promotion from other classes than had entered it direct: 1,331 compared with 1,295. The corresponding figures for Permanent Secretaries were respectively 7 and 27; for Deputy Secretaries 25 and 44; Under-Secretaries 82 and 131; Assistant Secretaries 393 and 326; and Principals and Assistant-Principals 816 and 762.

II

We consider the Civil Service today as a single entity but this was not always so. No description of it can be realistic which overlooks either the historical fact that there were once as many services as there were establishments and that it is on these that the principle of integration has been superimposed, or the political fact of the powerful continuing pulls in the direction of maintaining or reverting to the principle of severalness. The single service idea rests on a recommendation of the Northcote-Trevelyan report. It is strengthened by the financial and general responsibility of the Treasury, and this has been fortified by many decisions of specific application. Such was the creation in 1855 of the Civil Service Commission as a central recruiting, examining, and certifying body under Treasury regulation. The recognition of the Permanent Secretary of the Treasury as Head of the Civil Service followed not long afterwards, and was re-affirmed in 1919. It implies a single Service, as does the Order in Council of 1870 which established open competition and laid the foundations of a single grading system for the whole Service with interchangeability of staff between departments. Since the end of the first world war the general responsibility of the Treasury has been recognized by the creation of the establishment division and by acceptance of the principle of its concern with machinery of government. This was reinforced by the regulation that the principal departmental appointments require the approval of the Prime Minister after advice from the Head of the Civil Service, who was also charged with supervision of all appointments in general. Since the second world war both the post-entry training of officials and the organization and methods of departments have been given a similar emphasis in the structure and functions of the Treasury. So it might well seem that the single service principle and the unifying forces at the disposal of the Treasury had now reached their climax. But here, as in the constitution as a whole, the formal position does not represent the reality.

For there is another competing principle, that of ministerial responsibility which makes the political head of each department its complete master accountable for its every official and his every act; and beside the chieftainship of the Prime Minister and First Lord of the Treasury, there is the supreme authority of the Cabinet consisting of all such departmental heads and therefore reinforcing their individual authority. The official takes his orders from the head of his department and more often than not has spent his whole working life in the same department. While the Select Committee on National Expenditure in 1942 criticized the Treasury for failing to impress its unifying control more firmly on the consequent departmentalism, the best response is to be found in the words of the late Sir Warren Fisher.[1]

'The committee appreciates the progress made towards the creation of a single "service" inspired by common concern for the country's business. This ideal is still far from fruition but the advance from the scattered efforts of sixty or seventy more or less unrelated departments, each regarding its own affairs as all that matters, is nevertheless encouraging. In addition to an attitude of mind the "service" idea depends on a structure of control in which each department has a division for "establishments"— including, of course, "organization"—working closely with the central department. Finally, the committee admits the necessity of the Prime Minister's approval for all major appointments, on which he is advised by the official head of the Service. It should, perhaps, be made clear that this officer gives advice on appointments after discussion with the Minister concerned and after consulting his wisest colleagues throughout the service and that the Prime Minister, of course, can, and sometimes does, reject his advice.

'Although the Select Committee suggests that more changes might have been made in the inter-war period, it has obviously found in the records of that period a wealth of ideas for further reform. It appears to me that the committee has not altogether appreciated the practical difficulties of getting those ideas more fully adopted. I should like to refer, for example, to that most vital of all problems, the selection of men. Without the right man no paper scheme is of any use. Human judgment of men is

[1] *Manchester Guardian*, 28th November 1942.

fallible enough, but in the Civil Service there are additional handicaps. First, politicians rarely appreciate the fundamental importance of choosing the right man for a job without prejudice or sentiment. Both Ministers and official heads are apt to be prejudiced in favour of choosing men from their own departments. Secondly, the innate conservatism of officialdom struggles hard against all departures from custom. Thirdly, conventions long continued inevitably create vested interests strongly opposed to the appointment of men "out of turn". In short, "selection" as it is practised in efficient business concerns has in the Civil Service to contend with every sort of difficulty. The Chiefs of Staff of the three fighting Services have far greater opportunity in this sphere; their Services do not consist of innumerable independent "departments" with a score of Cabinet Ministers.'

Sir Warren Fisher himself would have liked further applications of the single service principle.[1] In the first place, while his influence over promotion was confined to the posts requiring the Prime Minister's approval—heads and deputy-heads of departments, and the principal establishment and financial officers —he would have liked it to extend down to the level of assistant-secretary. Secondly, he found that the Treasury advice to the Prime Minister was only too often overruled by the flow of influence through the departmental officials and Minister to the Prime Minister. Thirdly, he proposed that administrative grade officers should be initially appointed to the Service rather than to a department; be given a general training for a year; that the probation rule after the first two years should be rigorously applied with particular emphasis on general promise and capacity to appreciate the working of the machinery of government as a whole; and that after three or four years at headquarters he should be sent out to wherever he could be in daily and direct touch with the public of all sorts, with a subsequent spell in a different central or local government office, or other undertaking; and, if after all this varied training he showed himself unfit (however worthy) he should be retired on pension under Section 2 of the Superannuation Act, 1887. By such means Sir Warren Fisher thought that what he called 'the psychological vice of departmentalism' could be obviated; and he claimed that 'inter-

---

[1] *Sunday Times*, 14th November 1944.

play and exchange between all branches of the Civil Service, home and foreign, should be recognized practice'.

Certainly the single service idea has not been carried to such lengths as these. On the contrary, the chief reform of the last decade, that of the Foreign Service, has moved in the opposite direction. Undoubtedly this change has several great merits. It ends the narrow sectionalism within the Foreign Office, diplomatic and consular groups of officials, and it facilitates variation of experience among them. It also brings the Service as a whole more into contact with economic and social realities. It is a good principle too that Foreign Service officials may be retired before retiring age with proportionate pension, although the safeguards should be strengthened. For the power compulsorily to retire an official should never be capable of being used in such a way that it will discourage his independence of mind or his willingness to give the advice he judges best rather than that which he thinks least likely to be unfavourably received. But it must not be overlooked that, with all its merits, and these are due mainly to the previous backwardness of the Foreign Service, it does mean a victory for departmentalism, for it cuts off from the rest an important section of the Civil Service and diminishes the total possibilities of interchange.

Similarly, while recent criticism of the Treasury has alleged insufficient assertion of authority and general interference on its part in relation to departments, as well as too little initiative in its handling of such matters as the machinery of government, organization and methods, and the Civil Service, the strongest tendency in administrative innovation during the same period seems to have been in the direction of separatism and autonomy. Most clearly this is the case with the public corporations, of which the latest of a long line are to deal with atomic energy and commercial television. Partly there is a whittling away of a responsible and integrating authority, such as has been slowly built up in the system of the Treasury establishments division and the operations of the Civil Service Commission under Treasury regulation. Partly there is the creation of new public bodies beyond the reach of its influence, and into whose ranks there pass an appreciable number of hitherto dependant officials.

The reason for this paradox which risks returning us to the 'sixty of seventy more or less unrelated departments each regarding its own affairs as all that matters', the chaos in other words from which the unifying process of Civil Service structural development has largely rescued us, may well lie in the weaknesses of the central system to which Sir Warren Fisher's arguments point.

First, on recruitment, what is needed is a more elastic, less rigid treatment of the hierarchical principle, taking advantage particularly of the existence of the specialist or professional groups and of the newer administrators in nationalized services. As long ago as 1914 a minority addendum to the MacDonnell Report said: 'We believe that the creation of two large "administrative" and "professional" classes, within each of which and between which promotion would freely take place, would have the effect of improving the efficiency of all the officers concerned by increasing the variety of posts for which, as their individual capacities developed, they would, in fact, be freely eligible.'

Secondly, on training, while a beginning has been made with the nine officers at the Treasury now responsible for dealing with this, much more could be done in conjunction with the universities, by bringing together young officers from the civil and other public services, and by the promotion of individual creative research and training, to create a cadre of first-rate officers suited for all branches of public service.

Thirdly, on promotion, a lively and elastic policy conducted by a body of officials specially trained in the art of selection, ranging wide over all public employees, informed by the single-minded desire to choose well to the public advantage regardless of vested interest and departmental prejudice, while it could upset some routine expectations, might redound enormously to the general efficiency.

But, finally, such measures could only succeed if they were combined in a highly powered Machinery of Government department under the Head of the Service and attached to the Prime Minister. Again Sir Warren Fisher's answer to the Select Committee's suggestion of a Machinery of Government Secretary to the Treasury corresponding to the Financial Secretary is final. 'I strongly suspect', he wrote, 'that this politician would find himself merely a fifth wheel to the coach. His advice would not be accepted as final by Cabinet Ministers in charge of departments. They would almost invariably appeal to the Prime Minister, who in turn would not regard a junior politician as having the necessary experience or knowledge to advise. He would thus relieve neither the Prime Minister nor the Chancellor of the Exchequer, and, worst of all, he would be continually coming and going with the accident of promotion in politics.' No, the 'necessary experience or knowledge' can only be provided by a greatly strengthened body of officials. To this would have to be added a clearer assertion of the powers of the Head of the Service and a more definite assumption of authority by the Prime Minister whose department would then become the most important common service office of the whole system of government, providing a highly trained and carefully selected general staff for all branches of the civil and public services. What has been done by the Treasury's O. & M. officers—for improving the business arrangements for issuing passports or for the local government of Coventry—could be done at the higher levels of administration throughout all state activity.

Chapter 9

TREASURY CONTROL

By SIR JOHN WOODS, G.C.B.
(*Permanent Secretary of the Board of Trade*, 1945-51)

'OH, you must be very good at mathematics.' In the early 20s this was said to me more than once by intelligent and generally instructed people when, in reply to polite inquiry about my work, I said I was 'in the Treasury'. (I had regretfully to deny the compliment—my nearest approach to mathematical distinction lying in my having picked a Wrangler for a father.) There seemed to be, in those days, a widespread illusion that administrative work in the Treasury consisted mainly of calculations so abstruse and complex as to demand the attention of a first-class university mathematician.

It is possible, but I guess unlikely, that today more people are aware of the true nature of Treasury work, and particularly that central core of it which is commonly referred to as Treasury Control.

It is not my purpose here to describe in any close detail either the history or the mechanisms of Treasury control. Some background of fact is necessary; but interesting and important aspects of it will have to be omitted. I exclude altogether those functions of the Treasury which are primarily 'financial' in the narrower sense of that word; for example, the raising of money by taxation, or by borrowing, and currency questions. For the present I defer that rather special aspect of the Treasury function—the control of staff matters—Establishments. I am firstly and mainly concerned with the Treasury's duties in respect of the Supply Services—'Moneys provided by parliament'. These are key words. It is not possible to consider Treasury control of expenditure without first setting it against the background of parliamentary control of finance—the sacred principle which was established only after long years of constitutional struggle, and after centuries of procedural development in Parliament itself.

The first and fundamental point is that *any* expenditure requires prior approval by Parliament, an approval which is exercised in the main by the voting of the Annual Estimates for each department. (It is important here to note that the Estimates relate to annual expenditure; any voted money which is not spent in the financial year in question is surrendered to the Exchequer, and cannot be spent without further parliamentary approval.) Secondly, by the Appropriation Act, Parliament 'appropriates' the supply which it grants to particular purposes, these purposes being shown under the various Votes of the Annual Estimates; except in the case of Defence Votes money appropriated to one Vote cannot be devoted to the purpose of another Vote. Thirdly, Parliament, through the Comptroller and Auditor-General and the Public Accounts Committee, exercises a *post-obit* control or audit, to see that the money has been spent on the service for which it was voted, and for no other service, and that all expenditure has been duly authorized.

Parliamentary approval of the Estimates is in effect approval of the service for which the expenditure is required. This I call control in relation to policy. The appropriation and audit functions are directed more towards regularity and prudent administration. This important distinction is duly reflected in the operation of Treasury control.

The Treasury rôle in the control of expenditure must always be subsidiary to that of Parliament. Subject to this, however, Treasury control is both the precursor and the concomitant of parliamentary control; it supports, and is supported by, parliamentary financial procedures. For example, the Annual Estimates of the departments are first scrutinized and criticized by the Treasury, and cannot be submitted to Parliament without Treasury approval. Indeed, the Estimates for all civil departments are presented by the Treasury itself. If, as happens in the course of every year, more money is required for a particular service than was voted in the Estimates, the whole matter must be thrashed out and agreed with the Treasury before a Supplementary Estimate can be presented to Parliament. Upon the whole question of 'appropriation', for example in regard to the limits within which savings on one Sub-Head of a Vote may be applied to the purposes of another Sub-Head of that Vote (virement) the Treasury is the acknowledged authority, and to a degree itself holds delegated power from Parliament.

Similarly, the Treasury is much concerned with the audit supervision, exercised through the Comptroller and Auditor-General and the Public Accounts Committee, on such questions as whether expenditure was duly authorized, whether in certain circumstances it should have had prior statutory authority, whether a particular matter was prudently handled, in what circumstances were losses incurred. Indeed, the Treasury is invariably represented at meetings of the Public Accounts Committee —I have sometimes wondered, being present on such occasions, whether I was *amicus curiae*, junior counsel for the prosecution (the Comptroller and Auditor-General being my leader *pro hac vice*) or prisoner's friend.

The annual scrutiny of the Estimates is a most important event in the total process of financial control from the 'policy' aspect. It is on this occasion that the Treasury sees the whole expenditure of a department. It is, moreover, the occasion when the Treasury first has before it firm estimates of the total expenditure of all departments to be voted for the ensuing financial year. It is therefore the beginning of the process which balances the projected expenditure against the revenue possibilities, and is thus the first main plank of the Budget.

But scrutiny and approval of the Estimates is not in itself the main feature of Treasury 'policy' control. It is now established constitutional practice that departments must seek Treasury approval, whenever in the year the necessity arises, for every new item of expenditure, for any new service, for any change in policy which involves an increase in expenditure, or for any variation in the conditions on which expenditure may originally have been authorized. There is no express statutory basis for this rule. It is primarily a matter of custom, and constitutional usage, though it is implied in the Exchequer and Audit Department Acts of 1866 and 1921, and is stated in the Treasury minute of 1914 in the following terms:

'. . . It has however been the general practice of the Treasury in the past to require Treasury sanction of all expenditure out of voted money, and exception can only be made in regard to particular categories of expenditure of a special character, with regard to which free discretion has been given to Departments, subject to the limits of amounts specified in the Estimates or special limits laid down by the Treasury.'

The establishment of this rule has been a matter of slow development.[1] In the latter part of the nineteenth century the emphasis was more on 'regularity and prudent administration' than on 'policy'. The Gladstonian era, as Sir Edward Bridges has pointed out in his Stamp Memorial Lecture, stressed 'the saving of candle-ends'—good housekeeping. Nobody will deny the importance in today's conditions of good housekeeping in carrying out Government policy; but it is the policy itself which determines the major part of expenditure, and my conviction is that easily the most important element in Treasury control is the level-headed financial criticism of the policies, in themselves and in relation to other competing policies. It is probably true to say that the emphasis on 'policy' control, as defined in the Treasury minute quoted above, received a great impetus when, with the advent of the Liberal Government in 1906 (to use a phrase current in the Treasury itself in my early days there) 'the Treasury became a spending department'—or, with a nearer approach to accuracy, 'the Chancellor became a spending Minister'; when 'wise spending' stole a long march on 'letting the money fructify in the pockets of the people'.

But it would be wholly wrong to assume that the Treasury can, or wishes to, ride roughshod over the departments' policies on financial grounds. Such a claim would be in flat contradiction to the doctrine of ministerial responsibility. An attempt to exercise anything like a veto would bring a flood of appeals to the Cabinet, a great many of which the Chancellor would lose.

---

[1] We tend to assume, rightly on the whole, that Treasury control, like other good things in the Civil Service, dates from the Northcote-Trevelyan reforms. But it is important to realize that a coherent and articulate Treasury began to appear at the time of Godolphin and Lowndes, his Secretary of the Treasury. Though the main emphasis then was on revenue and taxation, there were glimpses of a slightly challenging interest in the expenditure of departments. This letter was written to the Admiralty about 1680:
'I have laid before the Lords of the Treasury the Memorial of the Commissioners of the Admiralty, and their lordships desire you to acquaint the said Commissioners that they will lay the same before His Majesty . . . in order to the receiving of His Majesty's direction therefrom for such supplies of moneys for the service of the Navy as can be spared for that purpose.'
See Trevelyan's *Ramilles*, pp. 163-7; and Miss D. M. Gill, 'The Treasury from 1660 to 1714', in the *English Historical Review*, October 1931.

In the interests of the Treasury itself, and of sensible financial administration, it is of the highest importance that the departments themselves should hold a high sense of financial responsibility and should be equipped with strong financial branches whose business it is to criticize, constructively but stringently, the policies and procedures proposed in their own departments before they are brought to Treasury notice at all.

It has been suggested from time to time that the finance branches of departments should be regarded as 'outposts' of the Treasury, and even that the Accounting Officer and the Principal Finance Officers in every department should be Treasury men. It is not the least of Sir Warren Fisher's great public services that he established firmly the principle of primary departmental responsibility for finance as well as policy—the two being inseparable. Economy and financial prudence, said Sir Warren, are not things to be imposed by the Treasury acting as 'the single-minded champion of solvency keeping ceaseless vigil on the buccaneering proclivities of the Permanent Heads of Departments'.

For my own part I regard a strong sense of financial responsibility *inside* departments as the first, and probably the strongest bulwark against the tides of financial carelessness or improvidence—against the fatuous doctrine that 'money doesn't matter'. Money, after all, represents resources—a fact of which no competent finance officer, inside or outside the Treasury, is unaware.

Departmental responsibility for 'finance' is now firmly marked by the fact that the Accounting Officer in practically every department is the Permanent Secretary. Historically, the main function of the Accounting Officer was to account; to concern himself with the formal regularity and propriety of all expenditure out of the Votes for which he is responsible. In modern times he must be prepared to answer for the efficient and economical conduct of the department as a whole, including the financial aspects of 'policy' questions. As Permanent Secretary and Accounting Officer he embodies in his own person the principle that responsibility for 'policy' and responsibility for finance cannot be separated.

But if this much emphasis is rightly to be put on departmental responsibility, what *is* the function of the Treasury? I refer later to its functions in co-ordinating departmental activity from the point of view of general economic policy. Apart from that, I would say, firstly, that however able the departmental finance officers may be, their thinking is and ought to be to some extent coloured by the general policy conceptions of their department. There is an important and legitimate place for the more detached outside critic. That is what the Treasury is. On the particular matter at issue the department will be expert—the Treasury inexpert. But the departmental man may also be an enthusiast: and enthusiasm, admirable quality though it is, sometimes runs away with discretion and judgment. The good Treasury man, I have always thought, ought to be very like a first-class common law barrister conducting a rigorous, but fair, cross-examination of an expert witness.

Secondly, the Treasury as a whole is aware of *all* the plans and proposals of *all* the departments. Maynard Keynes once said that in a perfect world no bad proposal would ever be put to the Treasury. Their function was to select the *best* from a collection of good proposals. It is not, alas, a perfect world. But there is solid truth in the observation. It was made obvious in the second world war. A proposal to build a new battleship might (and did) have to give way in favour of a tank programme, because supplies of armour-plate would not cover both projects.

The control of expenditure, I would say, has two main objects:

(*a*) to keep a watch on the total use of national resources for the purposes of government, as against their use for other purposes; and

(*b*) to see that the resources devoted to government use go to the most worthwhile purposes in the government sphere of activity.

I do not suggest that Treasury control of expenditure has always been an accurate instrument for achieving these ends. But I would hold that, imprecise though the instrument has often been, its operations have steadily become more refined, and have always tended to be beneficial from this point of view. One would not think ill of appendectomy as an operation because the surgical techniques of, say 1905 were crude as compared with those of 1950.

I have tried to describe the principal mechanisms of Treasury control as now established, and the general form of the relationship between Treasury responsibility and departmental responsibility in relation to expenditure. But I have touched only on the letter of the business. How is this system worked in fact by the people who have to work it?

It is not to be doubted that at times Treasury authority has been exercised somewhat *de haut en bas*, and with an air of intellectual superiority which was no doubt irritating, to say the least of it, to other departments.[1] Nor would irritation be lessened by the fact that for many years Treasury clerks were paid more than clerks of equal rank in other departments. In 1872 Sir Thomas Farrer, then Permanent Secretary to the Board of Trade, wrote to Mr Ralph Lingen, Permanent Secretary to the Treasury, in the following terms:

MY DEAR LINGEN,

I do not see why official war should not go along with personal peace and friendship; and official war is thus carried on with least detriment to the public service.

But I think you deceive yourself about the Treasury. Undoubtedly they have assumed more and more power; and their language is less and less civil and more and more dictatorial. And on the other hand the business is so far as I can judge less well done than it used to be. There is no public office where there are (so far as our experience goes) such delays and such blunders. It gives one the impression that young men without knowledge and experience have got into places too high for them. And there is undoubtedly an impression in the Service that the Treasury clerks take uncommonly good care of themselves, whilst they snub other departments.

You will find that these impressions—or similar impressions —prevail amongst the best men at this office, the Colonial Office, the Privy Council Office, the Admiralty, the Post Office, etc. etc., to an extent as it seems to me I have never known before. And I do not agree that this is a good thing. Economy and efficiency must be worked out from within and cannot be forced upon an office by the Treasury from without. And the wholesome state of things is when the best men in each office look to the Treasury as their helper against claims and proceedings which they better than anyone know to be improper. This

---

[1] I remember in 1920, when the Treasury staff had just been greatly enlarged—mainly by transfers from other departments—a famous if not notorious Treasury character commenting thus on the invasion 'Before the war the Treasury was regarded as the worst-dressed and the most high-spirited department of state. It might now be described as "*colluvies gentium*".'

is not the case now—and it is because I regard it as a most serious evil for the public service that I write to you, whom I have so long known and respected, exactly what I see and feel. On the subject of the Orders in Council there is war between us to the knife. I shall do everything properly in my power to expose and resist the injustice and evil which I think they will cause—and I hope to do so with temper, though the sense of injustice towards the Temporary Clerks and the annoyance of having all one's work for years upset sometimes makes it difficult for me to keep mine.

At any rate I don't mean to quarrel personally with you and am less likely to do so if you know what I think.

Believe me,

R. W. Lingen, Esq.   Yours very sincerely,

T. H. FARRER.

A gem of a letter. But though conflicts[1] still arise between the Treasury and departments I doubt whether any head of department would today feel the need to write quite so stiffly. For Farrer's view that 'the best men in each office should look to the Treasury as their helper' has more and more prevailed. And so has the converse proposition.

This was another of Sir Warren Fisher's conceptions. He came to the Treasury determined that superior attitudes of mind should not persist there; that positive and constructive financial work depended upon the joint efforts of the Treasury and departments. He held the view that the administrative class of the Civil Service should be looked on as a single *corps d'élite*, with plenty of movement from one department to another, and especially perhaps in and out of the Treasury. I am myself sure that this last view, though it has obvious dangers, is in principle right, and that having been put into practice (usually with discretion) it has proved its worth.

It is indeed of great importance for very practical reasons that the processes of Treasury control should be carried on in a spirit of mutual confidence and understanding between the Treasury and departments, and not as a matter of competitive outwitting of the other fellow. Government expenditure is very great; and

---

[1] I think they ought to arise. If, for example, there were never any differences between Their Lordships of the Treasury and Their Lordships of the Admiralty, I should conclude that there was something wrong in one, if not both, of the departments.

much of it arises in large blocks from great issues of policy—social service policy, defence, agriculture, atomic energy. Not only are the sums involved very large; such policies clearly extend in their consequences well beyond the limits of one financial year. Such consequences cannot be subsequently limited, except by a major act of government policy. And governments do not like reversing policies (their own, at any rate) on financial grounds.

Where matters of such moment are at issue it is imperative that the department should wish to bring the Treasury into the picture early—as soon as the department's own thinking begins to crystallize—so that the financial implications of the plan may be fully thrashed out inter-departmentally, with a desire on both sides to get the best answer in the public interest, before Ministers come to a decision. The same principle holds in relation to other policy matters, not so vast but yet important. There is in fact a rule of procedure designed to protect this position generally—that no memoranda may be submitted to the Cabinet, if any financial issue is involved, until the subject matter has been discussed with the Treasury.

The mention of major policy matters, the financial consequences of which extend forward in time, raises another question. The financial procedures of Parliament rest upon the *Annual* Estimates. The Budget is still the cash account of a single year. But whatever the formal procedure may be there is, rightly, a growing recognition of the need for the Treasury, for Ministers, and indeed Parliament, to take longer perspectives. The Budget statement and the accompanying White Papers, parliamentary speeches on legislation embodying costly continuing policies, more and more take account of costs looming ahead, and the forward picture generally. The Treasury itself, I believe, has begun a practice of periodically forecasting departmental expenditure for up to two years ahead of the current financial year. It is clear that if policies decided in 1954 (and earlier years) involved very large increases in the Budget of, say, 1957, this would (or should) greatly influence policy-making in 1955 and 1956.

When government expenditure is so high, when much of it arises in large blocks from major policy matters, when policy piles up large and increasing commitments ahead, it may reason-

117

ably be asked whether it is now sensible that *all* proposals for expenditure on new services, or extensions of existing services, should be submitted to the Treasury for approval, whatever the magnitude of the expenditure in question. Is it not possible that in present circumstances the Treasury expends so much effort on relatively minor, if not trivial, matters, that the large blocks of expenditure receive less attention than they should? Do they lose the pounds while chasing the pence? Do they niggle?

There is no simple or conclusive answer to this question. In the first place the Treasury does in fact delegate authority to departments on a fairly wide scale—for example it has been the practice for many years past in relation to Works and Buildings Votes (of course, within specified financial limits). The question is whether delegation could usefully and safely be carried further. One particular suggestion has been made. Departmental policies often include large programmes comprising a number of separate but related projects (for example, the atomic energy programme). Would it not be sufficient if the programme as a whole were discussed and settled with the Treasury *once and for all*, with the result that the separate projects constituting the programme need not be separately and subsequently submitted to the Treasury?

On all this I can only state a personal view. Treasury control is exercised in the light of historical doctrines, and under a body of established case-law, to which Treasury men rightly pay great respect. It is possible, I would say likely, that the great increase in the volume and complexity of government activities, and therefore of government expenditure, has not yet been matched by a sufficient adaptation of the rules governing Treasury control. I am myself an advocate of a move, but *not* a dash, towards more freedom for departments. The suggestion of greater freedom, as a general proposition, stands or falls by the standard of financial control within the different departments—and the standard no doubt varies considerably. Moreover, large programmes extending over two, or perhaps more, financial years often change very materially from the original conception. 'Once for all' Treasury scrutiny will not always be possible. Often it will be necessary in these days of hurry to put a programme to the Treasury before it is in final or comprehensive state. If so, the most the Treasury can do is to approve 'in principle' (two words which, in my experience, can cover a wealth of administrative danger). Clearly in that case further discussion with the Treasury will be required.

For these reasons the possibilities of wider delegation, whether in matters of minor importance or (even more) in relation to the constituent elements of large programmes, must be approached with caution and, I fear, piecemeal. No general formula is possible. But I think that the attitude of mind should tend in the direction of greater delegation, and should blossom into action whenever opportunity offers.

The control of staff matters, commonly called 'Establishments', is of course part, but rather a special part, of Treasury control. It is dealt with, authoritatively and as a separate subject, elsewhere in this volume. Here, therefore, I deal with it only in so far as it seems relevant to the general concept of 'Treasury Control'. In this field the Treasury operates, to a large extent, under statutory authority. For many years now every new department has been set up by statute; and the Act always contains provisions to the effect that the Minister may appoint such secretaries, officers and servants as he may, with the consent of the Treasury, determine; and that these shall be paid such salaries as the Treasury shall determine. The same principles are in fact recognized in those older departments not set up by statute. Thus the Treasury has control over numbers, grading and remuneration though recently, in relation to numbers and grading (but *not* remuneration) they have delegated considerable powers to departments. Superannuation is, by statute, under Treasury control; while conditions of service (hours of work, leave, etc.) are a matter for the Treasury by virtue of Order in Council.

But the Treasury's part in staff matters goes beyond the control of numbers, grading, pay and other conditions of service. It is for the Treasury to initiate and to focus any general legislation relating to the Civil Service, though in so doing they draw on the experience and collect the views of other departments. In consultation again with other departments, they take the leading part in the policy of recruitment and training and in the use of Organization and Methods techniques. The Whitley System of consultation and negotiation with staff associations is under the general guidance of the Treasury.

It is worth noting, because the matter is often misunderstood, that in questions of discipline the Treasury is *not* in a position of control. Discipline is a matter for the Ministerial head of the department advised by his Permanent Secretary though the Treasury must, of course, be consulted in any disciplinary case involving substantial losses of cash; and may be consulted in any case if the department concerned thinks it desirable.

The Permanent Secretary to the Treasury has personal duties as Head of the Civil Service in relation to the filling of certain senior posts in all departments. The chapter in this volume on establishments (to which I have already referred) explains that appointments to the two most senior levels of the Service require the assent of the Prime Minister advised by the Permanent Secretary to the Treasury. So, also, do appointments by the head of each department to the special posts of Principal Finance Officer and Principal Establishment Officer. The reason for this arrangement in the case of these latter posts is that the responsibilities of the Treasury in relation to expenditure and staff matters mean that they must be able to rely on strong and efficient officers in charge of these two aspects of departmental work. The procedure described above ensures that great care is taken in securing that this is achieved, and this function of the Permanent Secretary is properly to be regarded as an important element in the whole business of the Treasury control of expenditure.

It will be seen that the Treasury exercises great authority in the field of personnel and establishment matters, whether by reason of formal powers vested in them by statutes or Orders-in-Council, or because of the influence accorded to them as a result of long custom and practice.

It has been suggested from time to time that establishments control should be taken from the Treasury and vested in a completely separate department of state, e.g., the Civil Service Commission, enlarged for the purpose. I cannot believe that the possible advantages of such a plan would outweigh the grave disadvantages—and that for two main reasons. The first is that the cost of the Civil Service (about £500m. a year, including the pay of industrial servants, e.g. those employed in H.M. Dockyards) makes it a matter of high financial importance. The second is that because of its functions in the control of other expenditure, the Treasury has far the best knowledge of the work being done throughout the Service. The Treasury better than anyone else can relate the numbers and grades of people employed to the actual work to be done, and in so doing establish standards common to all departments.

The Treasury cannot expect to be a popular department; but it is in this field, probably, that it is least loved. That is, I think, inevitable. In the ordering of a great graded Service one is bound to incur the criticism of thinking too much of the grades, and too little of the people, of being too afraid of 'repercussions', of being remote and inhuman. No doubt the Establishments Department makes its mistakes. But I have noticed that its strongest critics in other departments, when required themselves to practice that most difficult art, establishments work, are apt to change their tune.

This is not the place to describe the various steps by which a broad economic viewpoint, as distinct from the purely financial, has worked its way into Government generally, and the Treasury in particular. But it is important to note the fact that when Sir Stafford Cripps became Chancellor of the Exchequer in 1947 he continued 'to exercise the co-ordinating functions in the economic field' with which he had been charged as Minister of State for Economic Affairs. The Central Economic Planning Staff then became part of the Treasury. Since then the Economic Section, formerly part of the Cabinet Office, has also been absorbed into the Treasury.

It is by now established that the Chancellor of the Exchequer has the leading part in framing and directing economic policy as a whole. He has at his disposal for the purpose a staff within the Treasury whose business it is to study the economy as a whole, how its resources are being deployed, by what changes or innovations of economic and financial policy they might be better deployed. In effect, therefore, the Treasury takes the lead in co-ordinating the policies of many departments, of which the principal are the Board of Trade, the Ministry of Fuel and Power, the Ministry of Agriculture, the Ministry of Labour, the Ministry of Transport and Civil Aviation, the Ministry of Supply—and the Foreign Office in its economic aspects.

It is no doubt arguable whether this general co-ordinating power, as well as the traditional control of expenditure, should be in Treasury hands. Certainly it imposes a heavy strain on the

Treasury and the Chancellor of the Exchequer. Critics may say, and have said, that it gives the Treasury too much power. For my part I believe the present arrangement to be right. Nor, I think, is this view a product of Treasury bias on my part. I have been one of the 'controlled' as well as one of the 'controllers'. An economic co-ordinator outside, and independent of, the Treasury will always be falling over the Treasury's feet, and *vice versa*. The broad economic view, and the broad financial view, cannot be disentangled. And I would rather run the risk of an over-powerful Treasury than bear the continual pull, and counterpull, of two overlapping Ministers, each claiming general and co-ordinating authority, with all the delays and frustrations which that would almost certainly involve.

I am not myself too frightened of an over-powerful Treasury. It is, I think, true that these recent developments have added much to the power and authority of the Treasury. The question is, of course, how is the power exercised. It is important (and I believe recognized) that in the general co-ordination of economic policy the Treasury should adopt something of an interdepartmental cast of mind. They should accept it that in their own fields the other economic departments have the right and the duty to initiate policy. The task of the Treasury is to co-ordinate these policies (which may of course have to be modified in the process) into one comprehensive and coherent policy. In so doing they will of course take the other Departments concerned into full consultation.

When all is said, these things depend ultimately on Ministers and their relative weights in Cabinet. A dominant Chancellor will get his way. A powerful Treasury machine at his disposal will enhance, but will not be the reason for, his dominance. And *vice versa* the machine will not of itself make every Chancellor a dominant figure. My own belief is that any sustained attempt by the Treasury to dictate would quickly create its own bow-wave of effective resistance.

I hope I have not given the impression that the processes of Treasury control, as now operated, invariably work with complete smoothness, and with no friction. Original sin has not wholly departed from Treasury Chambers—or from the other departments. But I do believe that over the last 30 years the frictions and irritations have been much reduced by a process of 'give and take' on both sides. The permanent head of a great department not long ago summed up the matter very neatly: 'The problem of Treasury control is how a body of men, with little detailed knowledge of the subject, is to control another body of men of, I hope, equal public spirit. . . . In general, of course, given the goodwill which is almost[1] invariably shown on both sides, it might be said of Treasury control—as the Frenchman said of the first gear-box: '*C'est brutal, mais ça marche.*' It would, I am sure, be a bad day for this country if the basic principles which underlie Treasury control as now established were abandoned, or undermined. As for the mode of operation, it is my belief that the process has become less and less brutal as the years have passed. None of these techniques stands still, and the processes of Treasury control, as of every piece of organization in the Civil Service, are under continuous review, and indeed modification. But I should be surprised, and a little suspicious, if ever Treasury control, like the gear-box, became hydromatically smooth.

[1] I like the word 'almost'.

Chapter 10

CIVIL SERVICE ESTABLISHMENTS AND THE TREASURY

By SIR THOMAS PADMORE
(Joint Second Secretary to the Treasury)

THE word 'establishments' is used in this title in the loose but comprehensive sense which it has come to bear in the daily jargon of Whitehall. In origin no doubt the establishment of a department was its authorized complement of staff. But we talk nowadays of 'establishments' as meaning the whole complex of official activity which arises out of the employment of civil servants by the Crown. We use the word to mean 'staff management' in its widest sense.

Except so far as it is necessary to an understanding of the present system and methods of Civil Service establishment work, I shall not concern myself with the historical development of that system. Nor shall I refer much to the formal machinery of law, of precept, and of powers (whether vested in the employing departments or in the Treasury) which lie behind the system. Rather am I concerned to give some general description of the state's present activity as the employer of over 600,000 non-industrial civil servants and of the relationships between the different authorities concerned; as well as to consider the interplay of forces that has given rise to the present system and some of its defects as well as its virtues. In short, what happens? Why? And what is right or wrong about it?

But first one may well ask why there should be anything special, or specially worth writing about, in Civil Service establishment affairs. What features distinguish its staff management problems from those of any other large employer?

A few other employers have staffs as large, or larger, and the problems caused by mere size are not peculiar to the Civil Service. Broadly, there are two things which distinguish the Service from other employments. First, there is the mere fact that it is a largely permanent government service. From this it follows, for instance, that limits must be placed on the political activities of its middle and higher grades. It follows, too, that it is subject to detailed scrutiny by Parliament, and all its establishment arrangements, including staff numbers and the salaries paid to grades and individuals, are public property and open to public criticism. Again, its arrangements for recruitment, promotion, transfer and dismissal must be such as manifestly to exclude the possibility of either political or private influence and of either favouritism or unfairness to individuals. These consequences have an all-pervading effect on the way in which the Service's establishment affairs must be handled, and they go far to explain the importance of the rôle played by the central and co-ordinating department. The question whether that rôle is best played by the Treasury, as in fact it is, or by some other authority, has been ventilated and examined from time to time in the past. It is briefly referred to in another chapter of this book (on Treasury Control) and I shall not attempt to discuss it further here.

Second, the Service presents a unique combination of unity and diversity. It is a single unified service, but its members serve under some scores of separate and partially independent employing authorities, and the duties which they perform are of almost limitless variety.[1]

Nearly everything that I have to say in the rest of this chapter would be found, on analysis, to trace back to one or other of the features just described, and it is the combination of all of them in a service employing such large numbers which gives to Civil Service establishment problems their special character.

Few people realize how various are the duties of civil servants. Most people think of civil servants as concerned almost wholly with forms and figures and other kinds of desk work. But not

---

[1] 'The duties [of civil servants] range from issuing a passport to selling postage stamps; from computing income tax liabilities to proving wills; from licensing imports to fighting the Colorado beetle on our beaches. Births and deaths, marriage and divorce, call them to action. They are concerned with pensions, health, explosives, bankruptcy, atomic energy, Domesday Book, nylons, the dollar balance and the Waterguard. There are not many forms of human industry not represented in the list, except perhaps sport, composing music, and telling fortunes.' Wyn Griffith, 'The British Civil Service, 1854-1954'.

only is the desk work itself highly varied in character and difficulty; more to the point, large numbers of civil servants do little or none of their work at a desk. The research scientist, the museum keeper, the agricultural adviser, the factory foreman, the telephonist, the postman, the designer of rockets, are all civil servants.

In its relationship with the people who perform all these duties the Crown has to do all the things that other employers do in relation to their employees: to recruit them, to train them, to set them to work, to give them instructions, to pay them, to settle and apply their detailed conditions of service, to supervise them, to discipline them, to select from among them for advancement and finally to pension them. How does it organize itself to discharge these tasks?

I shall not deal with recruitment at any length—not because it is not important, for it obviously is—but because I think it is already widely understood and because it is largely separable and separated from the other employer functions.

All recruitment of permanent staff, that is of staff who will normally remain in the Service at least until they reach the minimum retiring age, is the responsibility of the independent Civil Service Commission. To quote the Order in Council of 1920 'No person shall be so appointed until a certificate of his qualification has been issued by the Commissioners'. To this Commission, and to the Commission alone, falls the task of choosing from the candidates coming forward for appointment as civil servants. It is their business to maintain a flow of recruits of the standard and qualifications required for each branch of the Service; and to see that there is a fair field and no favour as between those who seek to enter the Service. But of course they work in the closest consultation with the employing departments whose needs for staff it falls to them to fill. The individual departments make their demands to the Commission for classes of staff employed in one department only; while for classes employed in all or a number of departments the Treasury collates and co-ordinates the separate requirements. Moreover, the framework within which the Commission operates is created with the assent of the Treasury as regards both the numbers of posts to be filled and the qualifications required of the candidates, so that when eventually, with the approval of the Treasury, the Civil Service Commission issues its regulations 'prescribing the manner in which persons are to be admitted to Her Majesty's Civil Establishments', this is the end product of a joint endeavour by all concerned. In short, the Treasury, the other employing departments and the Commission decide in consultation how many recruits of what types shall be sought; and the Commission finds and selects them.

But a civil servant—though a 'servant' of the Crown—is for practical purposes employed in and by a particular department and not by the government as a whole, or the Treasury, or the Civil Service Commission. Once he has been selected by the Commission and appointed by the department to which he is assigned, he becomes in effect an employee of the head of that department—usually a Minister. His 'contract' of service (which does not exist in any written form as a contract) is with the department, the head of which alone has over him the essential powers flowing from the employer-employee relationship—transfer, promotion, discipline, retirement. And though he is a permanent civil servant his appointment is at the pleasure of the Crown, which means that legally he can be dismissed at any time. In fact, however, he is not dismissed unless his service in his first few years, during which he is on probation, is unsatisfactory, or subsequently for serious misconduct or incompetence. He may, however, be compulsorily retired on pension if his office is abolished, or, if over fifty years old, in the interests of efficiency.

It follows from the fact that the various heads of departments are the employers of civil servants that the main part of the establishment work of the Service is discharged in and by the various departments. It is the employing department which assigns the civil servant to his duty, trains him for it, supervises him, pays him, watches his performance, promotes him and so on. In some of these things it acts as a wholly independent authority. In others it is under varying degrees of central control from the Treasury.

This control falls mainly into two parts; that which is concerned with the numbers and grading of the civil servants employed by departments and that which relates to their pay and other conditions of service. And, as with so many other aspects of government, one of the most difficult fundamental problems in relation to it is to know how to strike the best balance between centralized control on the one hand and on the other delegation of the power of decision, away from the centre, to the man on the spot. The evils of over-centralization are well enough known and they are the same in establishment matters as they are in many other activities of government: the proliferation of rules and regulations and the attempt to force varying circumstances into conformity with a general pattern; the complexity of paper work to which the rules give rise; the sapping of local initiative and the frustration of the sensible decision appropriate to the facts of the individual problem which are known only on the spot: in short, all those evils of 'red tape' which tend to make administration sluggish, inept and sometimes unjust. On the other hand, as I shall attempt to show later, the forces making for centralization are powerful and much if not all of the central control now operating in these matters appears to be virtually inevitable.

This question of centralization of control versus delegation of responsibility is answered nowadays in very different ways in relation to the two parts of the establishment responsibilities of the Treasury to which I have just referred, that is, control of numbers on the one hand and control of pay and conditions of service on the other. I will take first the control of numbers. Here the trend is towards what I will call control with a broad brush. Up to 1939 the nineteenth-century machinery of complement control retained most of its pristine simplicity. Only the Post Office had achieved any degree of emancipation. Elsewhere the Treasury concerned itself in the utmost detail with the numbers and types of staff, fixing the exact staff complement of every branch, division or section, and requiring its assent for any change whatever. This was true even in the case of staff at the most subordinate levels. It was still felt that only so could proper economy be ensured—and this in spite of the fact that long before the second world war steps had been taken (in large part on the initiative of the Treasury itself) to improve the efficiency and standing of the departmental branches concerned with establishment matters.

This system was necessarily abandoned during the second world war. Departments had rapidly to build up their staffs to undertake new or expanded duties; and new departments had to be created. Lengthy and detailed correspondence between the Treasury and departments to determine new staff complements would have been quite impracticable. Most of the departments of any size or importance were therefore given very large delegated powers in these matters to act on their own responsibility in accordance with the needs of the time.

No attempt was made after the war to return to the pre-war system. And in 1949 the decentralization of responsibility which had taken place of necessity during the war was in large degree formalized and made permanent with the issue of a circular on control of Civil Service establishments which was of great importance to the Service. It reorientated the relationship between the departments and the Treasury in these matters. This circular formally laid down the doctrine that the control of numbers in the Civil Service can only be carried out with efficiency by the Principal Establishment and Organization Officer of each department acting on behalf of its Permanent Secretary and Accounting Officer. For the first time the prime responsibility was laid firmly on the shoulders of the departmental authorities. As in the case of Treasury control of expenditure in other directions, the Treasury felt that the interests of staff economy would best be served if the Treasury were to concentrate on broad issues and to avoid matters of detail.

This meant that for major departments the Treasury would no longer concentrate its scrutiny on the addition of a clerk here and a typist there, or with the saving of individual posts or of small groups. Subject always to the over-riding control exercisable through its approval of departmental Estimates before their presentation to Parliament, it would largely content itself with controlling the total numbers employed by a department, leaving it to the departmental authorities themselves to deploy their staff in the way that seemed best to them in the light of their own close knowledge of the needs.

There are two main outward and visible signs of this new policy. The first is the global manpower budget fixed for each department for each half-year, and largely settled without going into great detail on the numbers of posts in individual divisions or branches, still less in each separate grade. When I say 'largely' I mean 'largely'. For one thing, the most senior posts continue to be settled individually between the departments and the Treasury. For another, the granting to departments of delegated powers to vary complements does not include sanction to undertake any important new function or to extend any existing function without Treasury authority. Further, it is sometimes the case that departments' proposals for their global total have to be discussed in detail if they are to be properly understood. The second important outward and visible sign of the new policy is the inspection of departmental establishments carried out on the spot by Treasury staff. In the same circular which announced the new policy of Treasury concentration on broad issues the Treasury reaffirmed its right of inspection and of access to departments—the right to go and see for itself—and particularly the right to submit particular branches and posts to closer examination if it should seem to it desirable to do so. Indeed, the circular laid great emphasis on inspection of work on the spot not only by the Treasury, but by the departmental authorities themselves; and it reaffirmed and underlined the departmental responsibilities for internal staff inspection, indicating that Treasury inspections would often be directed to examining the effectiveness of the departments' own inspections.

I think it is true to say that of all the responsibilities falling to the Treasury staff who go out among departments to see for themselves, probably the most important is that concerning the standards of grading of work. The greater the freedom of departments to control their own complements, the greater, obviously, is the necessity of ensuring that they are using appropriate standards of grading. Grading of work is an art, not a science, and except at the lower levels grading standards are not at all easy to define or to assess by yardsticks of general applicability. Thus the Treasury's responsibility here is crucial.

The Treasury has not changed its general objective—economy, efficiency and equity in staffing arrangements throughout the Service. The new arrangements are but new means to a familiar end.[1] Have they been a success, or have they given too much

---

[1] The problem is as old as civilization—as is illustrated by the following letter, written in A.D. 288 by Servaeus Africanus, a high official of the Roman administration in Egypt, to the district governors of Middle Egypt:

'. . . It is apparent from the Accounts alone that a number of persons wishing to batten on the estates of the Treasury have invented titles for themselves, such as controllers, secretaries or superintendents, whereby

rope to the spendthrift, the enthusiast and the empire-builder? They are only six years old, and one cannot yet give a final judgment: but the general opinion, both in the Treasury and in other departments, is that so far they have been a success. The delegation of responsibility away from the centre does seem, as was intended, to have improved what, for short, I will call the 'manpower consciousness' of departments, and this must have a good effect on the general standard of efficiency with which these questions of numbers and grading are settled. Because more responsibility is now carried in these matters by the departmental authorities much nearer to the work, those authorities and the Treasury are now pulling together rather than against one another. Of course, the 'manpower budgeting' which is done between departments and the Treasury still gives rise to differences of opinion. Indeed, it would be strange and wrong if it did not, for the Treasury must retain the right to call a halt when the departmental enthusiast shows signs of getting out of hand. (Sir Edward Bridges has in fact called this 'the heart of the business'.) Nevertheless, the Treasury does appear to be accepted by the departmental authorities much more as a friend, counsellor and co-ordinator than used to be the case. Certainly a great volume of interdepartmental correspondence has been abolished, to no-one's regret and with no apparent ill-effects.

Before going on to consider the other main aspect of Treasury control of Civil Service establishments—that of conditions of service—one point arises out of what I have said so far which is, I think, worth mentioning, though it is a big subject in itself and within the compass of this essay I shall be able to deal with it only very cursorily.

I have probably given the impression that as the central department the Treasury is vastly—and characteristically—in-

they procure no advantage to the Treasury but swallow up the profits. It has therefore become necessary for me to send you instructions to arrange for a single superintendent of good standing to be chosen for each estate on the responsibility of the local municipal council and to abolish all the remaining offices, though the superintendent elected shall have power to choose two, or at the most, three assistants. By this means the wasteful expenditure will be curtailed and the estates of the Treasury receive proper attention. You will of course ensure that only such persons are appointed to assist the superintendents as can stand public scrutiny. Good-bye.' (Papyrus 752.)

terested in numbers and complements in departments but in no way concerned with the individuals filling them, once they have been posted to a department. The official destinies of individual civil servants, I have said, are controlled by their employing department, and, I have implied, by the employing department alone. This is certainly generally true. But like most generalizations it is subject to some reservations. In fact the Treasury does not dissociate itself from what I might call the management of the people who make up the Service. It cannot do so for, as the central department, it must assume responsibility for endeavouring to ensure that the talent in the Service is used to the best advantage of the Service as a whole, and that its distribution is not left entirely at the mercy of the accident of the original assignment to departments. As many as thirty-five years ago this responsibility in relation to the very highest Civil Service posts was formally assigned, not to the Treasury as a whole, but to its Permanent Secretary. Since that time, appointments to the two highest Service grades, though continuing to be made by the Minister responsible, have required the assent of the Prime Minister, who himself is advised in these matters by the Permanent Secretary to the Treasury. And the object is precisely that stated above—to do everything possible to ensure that the ablest men go to the top wherever they may be found.

In recent times the effort to distribute ability and talent more evenly over the Service than 'natural causes' would do has been carried further. During the war it was, of course, obviously essential that the more stable or less pressed departments should release staff to those departments which inevitably expanded out of all recognition. What is accepted in war is not always accepted when the war is over. But although in peace-time there is not the same obvious necessity and therefore it is perhaps more difficult for departments to put the good of the Service before their individual interests, it is none the less accepted as desirable that the barriers between departments should not be absolute.

Thus, with the co-operation of departments, the Treasury of today seeks to identify the most promising individuals in the various departments, particularly, though not exclusively, in the administrative class, and as occasion arises to bring about the transfer of some of them to posts elsewhere where they can be employed to the greater advantage of the Service as a whole. It would be wrong to give the impression that such transfers are very numerous. They are not. But those that are brought about may have considerable significance for the efficiency of the Service.

The Treasury also runs a scheme—known as the planned interchange scheme—for the temporary exchange of administrative staff between departments with related functions, the object here being to widen the experience of the staff and so to increase their usefulness when they return to their own department. Again, the movements are not numerous but their effect may be real, if imponderable.

Nor are transfers between departments made exclusively at the higher levels. It is now accepted that there should be some machinery run by the Treasury, by which clerical officers can be promoted to be executive officers in other departments, the object being to maintain evenly over the Service a reasonable standard of promotion, and to avoid a situation where one department is promoting relatively mediocre people while elsewhere much better people are available. The machinery for attaining this objective is still in its infancy and no-one can yet be sure how it will develop. But its existence implies the recognition and development of a relatively new facet of Treasury responsibility.

After this digression I will now return to the second main aspect of Treasury control—its control over conditions of service. This is handled very differently from complements and numbers. Some civil servants are organized in classes common to all or to a number of departments. These are called 'Treasury classes' or 'general Service classes', and their conditions of service are the same wherever they are employed. Other civil servants are organized in classes (called 'departmental classes') which are peculiar to a single department and have their own conditions of service separately determined. Discussions with staff representatives are conducted by the Treasury in relation to the Treasury classes, and by departments in relation to departmental classes, while matters (such as superannuation) where the code affects all civil servants alike are discussed on the National Whitley Council. But as respects both general and departmental classes the Treasury retains control over all the main conditions of service—pay, superannuation, hours of attendance, leave, sick pay, and so on—and departments are required to obtain the assent of the Treasury to all that they do in these matters, for their departmental class as well as for their Treasury class employees.

This may indeed seem a formidable concentration of power in the hands of one authority. The process of centralizing these things in the Treasury was virtually completed after the first world war. The main development during the last few years has been a continual increase, first in the extent to which the Treasury seeks the advice and co-operation of departments before determining their policy, and second in the part played by staff representatives. In the following paragraphs I shall try to show why this general pattern—centralization, subject to constant consultation—is right and necessary.

The Treasury maintains a loose-leaf volume under the forbidding title of 'Estacode', in which the standing instructions in establishment matters are made known to the Service. This volume is now some four inches thick, and there is no sign of its getting any slimmer. It might be expected that not only the central establishment branches in the department but those who are concerned in the management of individual offices, large and small, would feel themselves oppressed and frustrated by this weight of regulation from the centre.

Generally speaking, however, this seems not to be so. There is a general recognition that a high degree of centralization in these matters is inevitable in present circumstances. Like many other employers—and in this the government can claim to have been in the forefront of modern changes—the government has long recognized the obligation to accept collective bargaining and all that it entails. Conditions of service can no longer be laid down from on high by an unfettered and unapproachable authority. They are hammered out in discussion and negotiation between employers and employed, and in a unified service they must meet similar circumstances in a uniform way and not be inconsistent with one another generally. This is not only because neither public opinion nor Parliament would be willing to accept capricious variations between the conditions of employment of servants of the executive employed on similar duties in different parts of the Service. It is also because, even if public opinion and Parliament might be prepared to tolerate divergences, one party to the collective bargain—the employed—would not. And this consideration is decisive, not only because there is a highly developed machine of collective discussion and bargaining in the Civil Service; but because behind that there has stood for some thirty years the right which the government has conferred on the great bulk of its employees to obtain rulings on emoluments, hours of work and leave from the Civil Service Arbitration Tribunal which, subject to the overriding authority of Parliament, are binding on the government.

The result is that all conditions of service are settled either directly with and by the Treasury or under its close supervision. And the departments on the whole appear to wish it to be so. For if, even in relation to purely departmental classes, departments were left to make their own collective bargains with their staffs, without co-ordination or supervision, they would inevitably find themselves causing great practical difficulties to one another. What one department might concede in negotiation would have effects on negotiations elsewhere of which it had no knowledge and for which it had no responsibility. This is the reason for the well-known Treasury preoccupation with the bogey of repercussions, which is so often a matter of jest and sometimes of real irritation. It is of course a preoccupation which can become an undesirable obsession. But it arises from the entirely proper doctrine that the state as a single employer cannot and should not arbitrarily deny to one what it concedes to another if both have equal claims. Only at the centre can the likely repercussions be estimated. Thus we cannot, I believe, have a unified service with staff consultation and negotiations unless there is also a high degree of central control and management of conditions of service.

But the Treasury does not nowadays attempt to do this part of its work without taking other departments into close collaboration. It does this in a variety of ways. On the biggest Service issues and problems Permanent Secretaries or groups of them meet at the Treasury for discussion and consultation, the initiative for such meetings coming usually from the Treasury, but sometimes from other departments. Standing bodies of Principal Establishment Officers of all departments meet regularly under

Treasury chairmanship for the same purpose. Central negotiations with staff representatives, whether under the auspices of the National Whitley Council or with individual national staff associations, is frequently carried out by an official 'team' which includes establishment officers or their representatives from a number of departments. And even when Treasury representatives appear in the lists alone, they have usually had on any matter of substance the benefit of prior advice from a number of other departments.

The machinery and methods of joint consultation and negotiation, both in the Whitley Councils (national and departmental) and between particular staff associations and particular departments, have developed and changed almost out of recognition in the last thirty years. In place of the formal, elaborate and perhaps rather sterile proceedings of some of the early Whitley Councils, most business is now done far more informally—especially, but by no means only, business done at the 'national' level. Standing or *ad hoc* committees—smaller, more practical and efficient bodies—have largely taken the place of the formal Whitley Councils and much business is transacted between individuals or small groups not dignified by the name of committee. Personal relations between representatives of the two 'sides' are almost invariably good and friendly.

This last fact, coupled with the sheer volume of business done and the give and take which this inevitably and rightly involves, may sometimes give rise to the suspicion that the staff side are 'in the pockets' of the official side. I believe—in fact I know—that this is not true. Give and take is on both sides. Certainly the contrary suspicion also exists—that the official side led by the Treasury at the national level is unduly timid in its relations with the staff side, especially in asserting the prerogatives and duties of management; this feeling is perhaps fostered by the official side's practice of keeping the staff side informed even on matters on which the latter do not claim to have any very active part to play.

In fact, the part played by staff consultation in the general running of the Civil Service is very big (we often find that it astonishes our friends in business and industry) and, to the great credit of the staff associations and their leaders, it goes at times well beyond looking after the interests of their members. This is largely a matter of attitude of mind. A significant example is to be found in the very full Whitley discussions which preceded and accompanied the reconstruction of the Service after the last world war. In those discussions the staff representatives never forgot the interests of those they represented; they would have been failing in their duty if they had. But they did not interpret these narrowly and they equally did not let their vision and their thinking become confined to them. In fact, I think it is true to say that that part of the constitution of the Civil Service National Whitley Council which includes among the objects of the Council the securing of increased efficiency in the public service is by no means an empty formula.

Even apart from this, staff consultation which is effective and is carried out in a spirit of co-operation can, by creating a fund of goodwill which flows from action by consent, contribute greatly to the maintenance and raising of general morale; on which in turn efficiency and output so greatly depend. These are perhaps platitudes. And it would be foolish to pretend that we are in sight of perfection in these matters, or, I dare say, ever shall be. But the Whitley system works—and pays more than respectable dividends to all concerned.

It would be wrong to make even a partial survey of establishment activity in the Civil Service without reference to the number of wartime and post-war developments, notably the new attention being given to Organization and Methods, to training and to staff welfare.

None of these things is new in itself; what is new is the way in which they are being handled and the amount of effort being put into them. For a long time government departments have had to think carefully how best to organize themselves, what methods to adopt. The pre-war social services, for instance, or the revenue departments were not developed and run without much O. and M. work going into the process—though no-one had heard the expression. Neither did the pre-war staff do their work without being trained for it. Similarly, staff managers at all levels increasingly interested themselves in welfare. But it is only in the last ten or twelve years that the Civil Service has begun to tackle this work deliberately, consciously, and to a substantial extent through specialist agents. And it is all being tackled in very similar ways. Specialist study of individual organizations and of the methods they employ is done mainly in and by the departments; while the Treasury handles those problems which are of wider interest (including the division of function between departments), co-ordinates O. and M. work in the Service generally, and maintains a common advisory service for those departments which are too small to maintain their own. Similarly the Treasury has set up a small training division which combines a co-ordinating and to some extent a supervising function with a limited executive function in the training of certain small categories of staff; but the bulk of training, even that which is given otherwise than by the prime method of doing the job under supervision, is carried out by the individual departments. In the case of staff welfare the Treasury's job is the handling of special welfare problems concerning the Service as a whole; and the co-ordination of the work and training of the specialist welfare officers appointed in the departments.

Does this system of staff management in the Service, the division of responsibility between the centre and the departments, between the specialist staff and the many thousands of 'general' managers at all levels of the machine produce the best possible results? Is the community in the end required to pay for a Civil Service which enjoys unduly favourable terms of employment or is unduly large? Those are questions on which it is hardly for a civil servant to attempt a public answer. The main conditions of service are however at the present time under review by a Royal Commission whose report will no doubt enable Parliament and the public to judge for themselves the terms of the Service's employment. The size of the Service— the point on which popular criticism mainly fastens—is governed primarily by the functions which government discharges and only secondarily by the system of control and management sketched earlier in this chapter. That system has been much modified in recent years. No-one will believe that it cannot be further improved. But it is quite possible to think that unless circumstances change very materially it is in its details rather than its general design and principles that further improvement will be found to be required.

Chapter 11

WHITLEY COUNCILS IN THE CIVIL SERVICE

By DOUGLAS HOUGHTON, M.P.
(*General Secretary, Inland Revenue Staff Federation*)

IN my long experience of unfavourable official replies I have seen nothing quite so dusty as the answer given by the Board of Inland Revenue to a petition from some wretched income tax clerks in 1890. It read:

'The Board will be glad if you will inform those clerks who signed the Petition that if they are dissatisfied with the weekly wages which the Surveyor of Taxes is authorized to pay, it is open to all of them to give one week's notice and to seek employment elsewhere.'

The clerk who actually forwarded the petition took the hint and went. The rest kept quiet for a while. These men should, of course, have known better than to fortify their claim to better wages by saying that local Clerks to the Commissioners of Taxes were lazy and overpaid. Under the comprehensive rules governing memorials only a 'respectful representation' could be received. Subsequent petitions were more wisely drawn up, with the result that ten years afterwards the Board consented to receive 'a small deputation' one Saturday afternoon.

That brought 'recognition'. Few associations of civil servants were 'recognized' at the turn of the century, and none at all representing classes common to the Service.

Associations of Post Office servants were given a form of recognition as far back as 1899, but their spokesmen had to be 'officers directly concerned'. This condition was relaxed a little later to allow of representations being made by the secretary of the Postmen's Federation who was not himself in the Post Office Service. It was not until 1906 that Mr Sydney Buxton announced that 'he was prepared frankly to recognize any duly

139

constituted association or federation of postal servants, and was willing to receive representations from the members or representatives of the Association through the secretary of the Association, whether or not he was a serving officer'.

No other Civil Service staff association then held such a favourable position. Nevertheless, other associations of departmental classes, such as Surveyors (now Inspectors) of Taxes, Officers of Customs and Excise, specialist and technical grades in the Admiralty and elsewhere, were able to make some headway. Grades common to the Service as a whole lagged behind. Efforts made to organize these civil servants for the purpose of making representations direct to the Treasury were largely frustrated by traditional official insistence upon these being made only to heads of departments.

This explains why the departmental associations were the first in the field and were developing relations with their respective departments before the general Service organizations were even formed.

At the time the MacDonnell Commission was appointed in 1912, there existed neither machinery nor means for those in common classes to get direct access to the Treasury. Even as late as 1915 I remember signing a petition to the Treasury for a war bonus, organized by the Civil Service Federation.

In the uncharted sea of future relations between staff and employer in public administration, the Commission offered no course or compass. It asked most of the questions but gave none of the answers. It suggested another committee of inquiry to supply them. But there was a war on; there was no time for more committees; it was a case of working things out as one went along.

As usual, the Post Office was several moves ahead of everybody else. While civil servants elsewhere were signing their petitions 'humbly praying' for a war bonus, a joint body of Post Office unions had asked for one and been turned down. The unions demanded arbitration and got it.

The arbitrator (Sir James Woodhouse) awarded a war bonus to lower paid Post Office workers. Other lowly paid civil servants, including boy clerks (of whom I was one) were denied similar treatment for well over a year. By the time the Civil Service generally got its first war bonus, the Post Office workers were pressing for a second round. This intolerable situation ended when the Prime Minister announced (November 1916) the setting up of a 'standing arbitration tribunal to decide during the war questions of wages arising between the government and its civil employés'.

For further deliverance the Civil Service awaited the coming of Whitley.

When the government set up the committee in 1916 under the chairmanship of the Rt. Hon. J. H. Whitley, M.P.[1] 'to make and consider suggestions for securing a permanent improvement in the relations between employers and workmen' they were not, however, thinking of the Civil Service. The trouble had been on the Clyde, not in Whitehall.

The committee's interim report dealt with 'the problem of establishing permanently improved relations between employer and employed in the main industries of the country, in which organizations fully representative of both sides were in existence'. The report described in outline the machinery of Joint (National) Industrial Councils, District Councils, and Works Committees, which it was recommended should be set up.

The second report of the committee (October 1917) dealt mainly with industries in which co-operation between employers and employed was less completely established. This report also contained a reference to state and municipal authorities and recommended:

'that such authorities and their workpeople should take into consideration the proposals made in this and in our first report, with a view to determining how far such proposals can suitably be adopted in their case'.

This part of the Whitley report was seized upon with enthusiasm by the Civil Service staff associations, and especially by those in the Post Office. Not only did it hold out hope of more general recognition, but of direct dealings with the Treasury on all-Service matters. The staff associations declared that any failure on the part of the government to practice what the Whitley report preached would weaken its authority as an advocate of peaceful and constructive relations in industry.

In 1918 the War Cabinet decided to adopt in principle the

[1] Liberal M.P. for Halifax, and later Speaker of the House of Commons.

application of the Whitley report with any necessary adaptions to government establishments 'where the conditions are sufficiently analogous to those existing in outside industries'. That was comparatively straightforward. The more difficult task was given to a committee presided over by Sir Thomas Heath, Permanent Secretary to the Treasury, which prepared a draft scheme for the application of the Whitley report to the administrative departments of the Civil Service.

This report, made in March 1919 and adopted by the government, drew attention to the difference between state and private employment and to the need for maintaining Ministerial responsibility 'unimpaired and unfettered'. It was therefore recommended that the proposed Joint (Whitley) Council 'should be purely consultative and should not be invested with any executive powers'. Further, the Heath Committee recommended that the scope of the joint bodies should be strictly limited to matters directly affecting conditions of service, thus ruling out all questions of organization, methods and management.

The government decided to put these proposals to a representative conference of Civil Service unions and associations for acceptance. This was held on 8th April 1919.

The Chancellor of the Exchequer (Mr Austen Chamberlain) attended in person and announced the government's readiness to adopt the Heath plan for consultative councils 'in the spirit and the letter', and promised that the government would 'do their best to make them work successfully'.

The sole and able spokesman of the staff associations, Mr G. H. Stuart Bunning, told the Chancellor that they could not accept a 'dictated constitution'. They were ready to co-operate on equal but not inferior terms. Moreover, they wanted Whitley, the whole of Whitley, and nothing but Whitley.

Faced with this united front the Chancellor yielded then and there. He did it so gracefully and so promptly that he left the meeting to the cheers of the conference.

Events then moved very quickly. A provisional joint committee was appointed to work out a modified constitution for Whitley Councils in the Civil Service. Sir Malcolm Ramsay of the Treasury was chairman, and Mr G. H. Stuart Bunning, vice-chairman. The committee began work three days after the historic meeting of April 8th and within a few weeks produced an agreed report differing in important respects from the earlier scheme of the Heath Committee.

The trouble with the Heath proposals was their obsession with 'the important principle' of ministerial responsibility and parliamentary control. Hence their conception of 'purely consultative' bodies with no 'executive powers', and the freedom of a Minister 'to accept or reject the conclusions of any Joint Council or Committee, even if they are unanimous'. Equal representation of the two 'sides' on the Joint Councils—another feature of the Whitley report—was rejected as a serious inconvenience to public business.

Provision for voting on these bodies was thought to be unnecessary: there would be no occasion for it. In short, the Heath Committee played up all the constitutional differences between joint councils in private employment and those in the public service. The Ramsay-Bunning Committee played them down. Their report, containing an agreed constitution for a Civil Service National Whitley Council and a 'model' constitution for Departmental Whitley Councils, got closer to the form and pattern of joint councils in industry. They dressed up Sir Thomas Heath to look more like Mr J. H. Whitley.

There was to be equal representation of the two sides ('official side' and 'staff side'). The chairman was to be a member of the official side; the vice-chairman a member of the staff side. But still no voting—'the decisions of the Council shall be arrived at by agreement'. All the difficulties of ministerial responsibility and parliamentary control were swept aside into the simple provision that decisions of the National Whitley Council 'shall be reported to the Cabinet and shall thereupon become operative'.

The objects and functions of the proposed National Joint Council for the Civil Service were taken, mostly without change of language, from the corresponding statement of purpose of the industrial Whitley Council. These were ambitious, and in parts grandiose. They included 'determination of the general principles governing conditions of service, e.g. recruitment, hours, promotion, discipline, tenure, remuneration and superannuation': and 'proposed legislation so far as it has a bearing upon the position of civil servants in relation to their employment'; and 'means for securing to the staff a greater share in and responsibility for the determination and observance of the conditions under which their duties are carried out'.

Neither the staff associations nor the Treasury were ready for all of this, but it was 'Whitley', and nothing less would do.

Red Tape, the magazine of the Civil Service Clerical Association, claimed that 'civil servants have acquired a new status by this Report'. More boldly it said—'The organization and control of the Civil Service will henceforward be the joint task of the representatives of the staffs and representatives of the State as employer. . .'

Yet in the background the British Constitution stood where it did. Parliament was still supreme. The Chancellor's control over the Treasury, and the Treasury's control over departments remained intact. While the Heath Committee may have been unduly concerned with the hypothetical dangers of permanent officials serving on these joint councils, and possibly committing themselves to agreements which their Ministers might not accept, the constitutional theory of the Ramsay-Bunning Committee was equally naïve, if not positively misleading.

The provision for agreements to be reported to the Cabinet and thereupon to become operative implied far too much.[1] It soon became clear that the substance of the matter was very different.

The official side is indivisible. That is the fundamental point of the whole Whitley system in the Civil Service. It may have been imperfectly understood by its founders. Agreements are not reached and subsequently reported to Ministers. They are authorized by Ministers before they can be reached.

Any hopes the Civil Service may have had that the introduction of Whitley Councils would separate the government as employer from the government and Parliament as the wielder of sovereign power were soon dispelled.

Two big issues were virtually barred from National Whitley Council negotiations from the start: the claim for equal pay for women, and the staff claim for the removal of certain restrictions on the civil rights of civil servants. Both were held by successive governments to be matters of high policy. In 1927 the government imposed a cut in the cost-of-living bonus payable on basic

[1] The Tomlin Commission (1929-31) described these words, in paragraph 495 of its Report, as 'a mis-statement of the position'.

salaries to senior civil servants. This action was taken quite suddenly and arbitrarily following some unfavourable comment on the subject in debate. When criticized for it, Mr Winston Churchill, then Chancellor, declared that:

'. . . while the government have every intention of continuing to make the fullest possible use of the machinery of Whitley Councils in Civil Service matters when it is appropriate, they cannot in the exercise of their responsibility to this House surrender their liberty to take such action as may appear to them in any case to be required in the public interest. This discretion is a recognized condition of the establishment of Whitley Councils in the Civil Service and the government do not intend to waive it'.

No government is ever likely to do so, but when government is employer and the executive rolled into one (as well as the political party commanding a majority in the House of Commons) it must be careful in its use of the overriding power. This is made the more imperative by the strong tradition in the Civil Service against the use of the strike weapon. If Civil Service unions are to rely solely upon persuasion and argument in support of their claims, and have to treat with an employer who is also the government, there is a pretty strong case for appointing an umpire. Hence the need for a permanent arbitration tribunal to settle disputes, a royal commission every twenty years or so for a general check-up, and the occasional committee in between to offer guidance on the more controversial current problems. It is curious how the government of the day failed to see that.

In 1922 the government came to the conclusion prematurely and quite unwisely that 'the conditions which led to the establishment of the Civil Service Arbitration Board . . . have been entirely changed by the formation of Whitley Councils . . . and the government have come to the conclusion that the continuance of the present arrangements for compulsory arbitration are inconsistent with, and to some extent militate against, the development of these Councils on best lines'.

Strong protests against this step eventually led to the restoration of arbitration machinery in 1925, when agreement was reached on the use of the Industrial Court for the purpose.

Latterly a special Civil Service Arbitration Tribunal has once more been used. Therefore, for the past thirty years, except for the short break between 1922 and 1925, compulsory arbitration has existed as a means of settling disagreements on the Whitley Councils as well as other disputes. The principle of 'compulsory' arbitration (that is to say, obligatory at the request of either side) is not generally acceptable to industrial trade unions, except in war-time. It was expressly demanded by the Civil Service associations. Having eschewed the strike weapon they would be almost powerless without it.

A general review of the working of arbitration and of Whitley Councils in the Civil Service was not within the terms of reference of the recent royal commission under the chairmanship of Sir Raymond Priestley. Had it been otherwise, what would staff sides of Whitley Councils, and official sides for that matter, have been saying recently in evidence to the royal commission on these subjects? In my opinion, very little; less today than they said to the Tomlin Commission twenty years ago, but expressing even greater satisfaction with existing arrangements. On that occasion members of the official side did most of the talking and most of the complaining. Their criticisms of cumbersome machinery have been largely met by the improvisations adopted during the war and by their continuance since.

In recent years, especially since 1939, the formalities of joint meetings and other constitutional procedures, which heads of departments found so tiresome, have been rarely used. The full National Whitley Council has only met twice in the last fifteen years! Most of its members have never been called to a meeting. Many departmental Whitley Councils also meet infrequently. This is no sign of diminished activity or usefulness, or of any falling off in the 'spirit' or practice of Whitleyism. Just the reverse: the volume of business has grown, the pace has quickened; all of us in this field of joint consultation are up to the eyes in work. We get through it as best we can. Both sides have found a satisfactory working arrangement within the framework of the original objects, constitution and composition of the Whitley Councils.

The staff sides of the National Whitley Council and of departmental and subsidiary Whitley Councils continue to meet regularly, as they have all along. The 27 members of the national staff side function as a kind of federal executive. They meet at least every month: a general purposes committee meets once or twice a week.

The staff side retain the formalities of their own separate function in the working of the Whitley machinery more perhaps than the official side, and for obvious reasons. The staff side gets its policy and authority from its member bodies and it cannot take undue liberties with them. Nevertheless, it tends to delegate considerable power to its general purposes committee which consists of the general secretaries of the half-dozen most influential staff associations.

When meetings are necessary on an especially important problem, *ad hoc* arrangements are made. For instance, discussions on the future recruitment of the clerical class and the provision of further opportunities for temporary clerks to compete for permanent posts are now taking place on a joint committee consisting of the general purposes committee of the staff side (specially enlarged for the purpose) and an official side containing establishment officers of several large departments, a Civil Service Commissioner, and the Treasury. The joint committee which agreed upon the introduction of equal pay for women in the Civil Service in seven instalments was composed on the official side of senior Treasury officials. The only departmental voice on the official side came from the Post Office, where particular difficulties existed in applying the principle of equal pay to such classes as women telephonists, whose conditions of service as regards liability to do night duty differed from those of men.

The more important agreements are signed on behalf of the two sides, but formal ratification by the full Council has long been dispensed with. A host of day-to-day or minor matters are disposed of by verbal agreement or by correspondence. These exchanges may be conducted by the staff side chairman (Sir Albert Day) who has for some years devoted his whole time to his duties, and who is a paid officer of the staff side. Many things are 'left in the hands of the chairman' which would have occupied the time of joint committees years ago. The staff side chairman can do much personally and informally to explore the possibilities of a situation and to prepare the way for a more formal approach.

Whitleyism in the Civil Service was given a new and lasting significance during the second world war. Staff associations in the Civil Service, like those in the wider trade union movement, dealt with their war-time problems with responsibility and courage. They now enjoy, somewhat modestly perhaps, the higher prestige and influence acquired by trade unions generally. Whitleyism has been extended and strengthened in the favourable conditions of post-war Britain. A new generation of 'Whitley-minded' Treasury and departmental establishment officers has arrived. They have dispensed with much of the old form, with staff side consent, because formal constitutional sanction is no longer necessary to most of what is done in the name of Whitley. The new machinery of negotiation has been improvised within the structure of the old. It is more flexible, in some respects more comprehensive, and is adaptable to almost every requirement. It does its job to general satisfaction. As mutual confidence has grown much of the elaboration of the original constitution has been virtually dismantled in favour of more businesslike methods. The personal contribution of Sir Albert Day, chairman of the national staff side, to this agreeable state of affairs is very great indeed.

Whitleyism has not perhaps lived up to the full grandeur of its original objects and functions, though the Tomlin Commission on the Civil Service (1929-31) corrected (in chapter XIII of its report) some of the possible misconceptions of those articles of the constitution which 'might lend some colour to the view that the Council is something more than a body to facilitate the discussion of matters affecting the conditions of employment of civil servants'.

It has, however, brought about a more contented Civil Service, which is certainly what both sides wanted. The cumulative total of constructive work done by Whitley Councils at all levels during the past thirty-five years is enormous. These Councils, together with all other forms of contact between staff and official sides, fulfil their main purpose, which is to fix pay and decide conditions of service generally by agreement with the staff. On pay questions, however, it must be admitted that use made of the machinery of the Whitley Councils fluctuates according to the nature and circumstances of the claim. War bonuses for the Civil Service were granted by agreement on the National

Whitley Council. So was the agreement to consolidate bonus and pay. Thereafter the associations representing the main grades and classes made separate claims, but all came together again to conclude an all-service 'pay addition' in 1952. Similar central discussions were refused by the official side in 1953 when a series of sectional claims went to the Arbitration Tribunal. In 1954 the Post Office unions sought separate pay negotiations, and by so doing made it impossible for the staff side as a whole to act together. The resourcefulness of the rest of the associations in joining together in a 'consortium' for the purpose of collective negotiations with the Treasury obviated a repetition of earlier disarray on both sides.

On many matters relating to conditions of service common to several or all sections of the Civil Service the central machinery of the National Whitley Council is invariably used. These include superannuation, hours of work, holidays, removal and travelling expenses, pay increases on promotion, recruitment, principles of promotion, and so on.

In some fields of joint endeavour envisaged by the founders of Whitley Councils there has been little progress. Experience has shown that there is practically no scope for discussing matters of government *policy* even though they may have direct bearing upon working conditions, for example when heavy overtime may be called for to complete the government's timetable for the issue of new pension books, or the completion of income tax recoding under P.A.Y.E. The first the staff hear of these things is after the Minister's statement in Parliament.

In general it is not the job of the Whitley Councils to try to run departments or to usurp the functions of those responsible for administration. They can do a great deal to help with suggestions and ideas, and staff sides may come near sometimes to grafting themselves on the structure of management. It must not be forgotten, however, that they are all the time representatives of the staff: they are the spokesmen of trade unions. They have no other right to be there. All the complex and controversial questions of what are the functions of trade unions in a changing society trouble them just as much as they do the National Union of Railwaymen and others. The joint production committee in industry and the uneven results of joint consultation at works and factory level offer no outstanding examples of what should be happening on Civil Service Whitley Councils.

The original constitution and functions of Whitley Councils have needed no substantial alteration since. There has been no general desire to widen their scope. Whether at some time in the future the elaborate constitutional structure, now largely in abeyance, should be reviewed and simplified is not one of our pressing thoughts.

Larger than any of these constitutional issues is this challenging question—is the Civil Service recruiting the people it needs, and paying the salaries to get them? Are the Whitley Councils—supplemented by the Arbitration Tribunal—doing more than deal with 'pay claims', formulated on traditional lines, within the general limitations of the economic and social policy of the government of the day?

What about differentials and comparative rewards? Staff sides and staff associations must find the most acceptable common denominator. They are there to do the greatest good for the greatest number. Whitley Councils can never give the Civil Service a shake-up: they can never deal in debits and credits: staff sides won't let them. It takes a two-thirds majority on the national staff side to carry the day on any matter of policy. Relatively small vested interests can combine to frustrate what may be to them an undesirable change. A majority of the national staff side representing overwhelming numbers of civil servants failed under this rule to carry acceptance of Treasury proposals to re-arrange hours and leave allowances in 1949.

The setting up of the Priestley Commission, at present sitting, to deal with pay and conditions of service (and the Tomlin Commission of 1929-31) is an acknowledgment that Whitley Councils have their limits. These may not be put there wholly by the staff representatives and the members at the back of them. The government may themselves be in genuine doubt about their own policy and outlook, They may also desire the authority of a royal commission to fortify them in what they do or decline to do.

There is no cause for lament. Mr Whitley would say, I have no doubt, could he be recalled for an opinion, that his joint councils were not intended to re-shape, reorganize and recruit a Civil Service of three-quarters of a million people, but to keep the peace and make people happy in their work.

Chapter 12

THE SOCIAL BACKGROUND OF THE HIGHER CIVIL SERVICE

By R. K. KELSALL
(*Senior Research Officer, London of School of Economics and Political Science*)

WHAT, it may be asked, can one hope to gain by an inquiry into the social background of higher civil servants? Sir Warren Fisher, in his evidence before the Tomlin Commission, was highly critical of those who sought to raise this issue. 'When I am looking at a fellow, really I am not concerned with what his father was: I am concerned with what he is.' What possible bearing has a matter of this kind on the efficiency of the service?

The answer to such a challenge could take several forms. In the first place, the ordinary citizen knows that, since the reforms of the 1870s, recruitment to the main branches of the Service has been by open competition amongst those with the requisite education and abilities. He therefore naturally expects that, by this time, the proportions in which higher civil servants are drawn from the several social strata will roughly correspond to the relative size of those strata. If the figures suggest that this is not so, he is likely to conclude that the blame lies with recruitment policy or the educational system. He is unlikely to be readily convinced of the importance of other possible factors, such as the uneven social distribution of (a) the basic qualities needed for success in administrative work, or (b) aspirations to enter the administrative class. It is in accordance with the traditions of a democratic community that he should be furnished with such figures even if, in common with other published statistics, they are open to a variety of possible interpretations.

Apart from the need to show how the theoretical equality of opportunity to enter the public service is translated into prac-

151

tice, a second justification for such an inquiry lies in the possible loss of efficiency in the higher branches of the Service resulting from a relative failure to tap the latent abilities of those of humble origin. We know, for example, that recent investigations in Scotland and elsewhere have shown that some two-thirds of the children with a high level of measured intelligence have fathers in the manual and routine non-manual categories. It is also generally agreed that a high level of measured intelligence is one of the qualities needed by those in the most responsible Civil Service posts. If, therefore, in the filling of these posts there is a marked under-representation of the lower social strata, it is a reasonable inference that the interests of the Service will suffer, unless the other qualities required are distributed very differently from this one.

A third justification for studying the social background of higher civil servants also has a bearing on the question of efficiency. Although members of the British administrative class have often been praised for their incorruptibility, their willingness to subordinate personal interest to that of the Service, their loyalty to Ministers, their conscientiousness and industry, their tact, personal charm and literary facility, they have also been severely criticized for being cautious, for lack of drive and personal vitality, for having a negative attitude of mind, for smugness and complacency, for being out of touch with working class problems and ignorant of recent advances in both the natural and the social sciences. These faults, as many of the critics have pointed out, are characteristic of those with a middle-class upbringing and a public-school education. No doubt a higher Civil Service predominantly recruited from the working class would have faults of its own. Nevertheless, if certain attitudes of mind tend to be associated with particular types of social origin, it is possible to argue that something would be gained if those in controlling positions in the Civil Service roughly reflected, in their family and school background, the pattern of society as a whole.

In all of this it should perhaps be emphasized that no one really expects the correspondence between the social origin distribution of those inside and outside the Service to be a very close one. The sons of unskilled labourers, for instance, whatever their innate abilities, normally find so many obstacles in the way of social advancement (inability to delay their entry to paid employment, lack of knowledge of opportunities or absence of parental aspirations to grasp them, the pressure to conform) that they always tend to be seriously under-represented in recruitment to any profession. Although it represents a 'perfect' recruitment situation unlikely ever to be realized in practice, however, the relative proportions of adult males in the various social strata in the population as a whole (on an occupational status basis) can legitimately be used as a yardstick to measure the extent to which different professions are being narrowly or widely recruited at different points in time. Moreover, the relative stability of the proportions of adult males in the broad occupational categories at successive population censuses makes it possible to use the 1951 census figures for this purpose, even when the occupations of the fathers of the people concerned actually relate to much earlier periods.

Even if these arguments are accepted, however, doubts may be felt as to the need for a fresh inquiry. Have the Civil Service Commissioners not published, for very many years past, particulars of the education of successful candidates at open competitions for entrance to the administrative class? And have these figures not been widely accepted as showing the changing social origin pattern of that class of the Service? Both these statements are true; yet the usefulness of these particulars for our purpose is seriously impaired by two circumstances. First, they relate to the last school and the university attended and these, by themselves, do not form a very satisfactory index of social origin. Secondly, open competition entrants do not constitute the whole of the administrative class or of the higher Civil Service, nor are they in any sense random samples of these universes.

The extent to which account must be taken of other types of entrant if we hope to obtain a representative picture may be shown by two examples. Of every hundred new recruits to the administrative class in the recent past (grouping together those who first entered that class as assistant principals, principals and assistant secretaries), about 50 have been open competition entrants, 43 have been promoted from the general or departmental executive classes (either by limited competition or otherwise), and the remaining 7 have been transferred from other classes or from the Foreign Service. Of every hundred higher civil servants (of the rank of assistant secretary or above) in 1950, 44 had entered the administrative class by open competition or its post-1918 equivalent, 14 by other forms of direct entry from outside (including the subsequent establishment of wartime 'temporaries'), 36 by promotion from the ranks, and the remaining 6 by transfer from other branches and other services. Whether we are concerned with the higher Civil Service as it is today or as it will be in ten or twenty years' time, therefore, it is misleading to generalize about social origins on the basis of open competition entrants alone.

The data upon which this article is based were obtained as part of a wider study by the present writer, the results of which have recently been published. For the detailed figures, for their statistical validation, and for a description of the very many sources from which the material was assembled, the reader must be referred to the main publication.[1] We may begin by comparing the social origins of those members of the administrative class *above* the rank of assistant secretary in 1929, 1939 and 1950. Subsequently the open competition entrants among the 1950 group can be compared with the successful candidates in the open competitions of 1949-53.

For our first comparison we have 121 people of appropriate rank in 1929, 179 in 1939, and 331 in 1950. Only 7 per cent of the 1929 group were the children of manual workers or domestic servants; the corresponding percentages in 1939 and 1950 were 10 and 17. At the other end of the social scale, 8 per cent of the 1929 group had fathers of independent means, and this fell to 3 per cent at the two later dates. The church, medicine, law and teaching between them contributed about a third of the total in 1929, and rather more than a quarter by 1950. To relate our Civil Service data to the social status groupings of the population as a whole, we may take as a rough yardstick the occupational distribution of the 1951 adult male population between the Registrar-General's five social class categories. Category 1 and 'no gainful occupation' combined account for only 5 per cent of the male population of Great Britain aged 20-64; they include those in the main professions (other than teaching), owners and managers of businesses

[1] *Higher Civil Servants in Britain*, published in May 1955.

(other than those engaged in wholesale or retail trade and certain other activities), Civil Service administrative and other higher officers, and secretaries of institutions and charities. The corresponding proportions amongst the fathers of our senior civil servants are about 40 per cent in 1929 and 1939, and 32 per cent in 1950. Category 2, 'intermediate occupations', includes teachers, farmers, those in the executive classes of the Civil Service and their counterparts in local authorities, owners and managers in wholesale and retail trade and certain types of transport, draughtsmen and social welfare workers. This second category contains 15 per cent of the adult males compared with 47 per cent of the fathers of our 1929 group, 42 in 1939 and 40 in 1950. When we come to category 3, 'skilled occupations' (comprising clerks, shop assistants, other ranks in the Forces, postmen, foremen, skilled manual workers) the position is, of course, reversed. More than half of the adult males in the population come into this class, but even in our 1950 group, fathers of this occupational status account for less than a quarter of the total; the proportions had been 16 per cent in 1939 and 12 per cent in 1929. Finally, categories 4 and 5, 'partly skilled and unskilled occupations', include 28 per cent of the adult males in the country as a whole, but only 3 per cent of the fathers of our 1950 and 1939 groups, and none of those of the 1929 group.

In explaining differences of this order of magnitude between the social origins of higher civil servants and the social status distribution of the adult male population, there can be no doubt that the principal factor involved was the failure of the educational system to provide adequate opportunities for talented children in the main social strata to reach the requisite standard of formal education. In the competitions for entry even to the lower classes of the Service (from which there were very limited opportunities of promotion to the higher division or administrative class) educational tests militated against the chances of those with only the minimum elementary schooling. Above all, however, the competition for entry to the highest class of the Service had, from the beginning, been of such a character that virtually only those whose parents could afford to give their sons an expensive education could reasonably hope to succeed. From 1870 to 1914 the majority of those who came in by this, the main route of entry, had spent three years or more at an Oxford or Cambridge college followed by a further six months or so at one of the London 'crammers'. There were, of course, exceptions. Sir John Anderson, who rose to be Permanent Under-Secretary for the Colonies in 1911, completed what must have been a relatively cheap education at Aberdeen University. Sir Albert Flynn, who became Director-General of Finance at the Ministry of Pensions in 1916, was successful in the open competition without ever going to a university at all. The number of such cases was, however, very small; and in the 1920s a step was taken which tended to increase the difficulties of those few whose intellectual brilliance and skill in written examinations had hitherto compensated for their social handicaps. An interview became, for the first time, an integral part of the open competition for entry to the administrative class; and the proportion of the total marks allocated to this *viva voce* often made it the factor determining a candidate's success or failure. In the description of the purposes for which the interview was introduced there was, of course, no mention of social origin or related issues. It was a question of alertness, intelligence and intellectual outlook, of presence of mind and nervous equipoise. Inevitably, however, there was the possibility of social bias, conscious or otherwise. Moreover, the manners and general bearing of the public school boy might be a valuable asset in his subsequent career as a higher civil servant; to this extent, giving him an appropriately better mark might seem consistent with the best interests of the Service, even though such a policy could not, in a democratic society, be openly avowed. The whole question of the extent to which the pre-war interview tended to prejudice the chances of those with the wrong kind of educational and social background is highly controversial, and is discussed at some length in the main study. There can be little doubt, however, that the change in recruitment policy represented by the introduction of a *viva voce* played a significant part, though subsidiary to the basic deficiencies of the educational ladder, in restricting the range of social strata from which higher civil servants were drawn.

In spite of this, as we have seen in comparing the position in 1929, 1939 and 1950, these officials tended to come to a progressively decreasing extent from groups of superior social status. The changes were not, however, revolutionary in character. In particular, the obstacles in the way of the sons of unskilled labourers reaching high office were clearly so formidable that even by 1950 it rarely occurred. Nevertheless, it is both interesting and important that as many as 17 per cent of the senior officials in 1950 should have been the children of manual workers and domestic servants. Some three-fifths of those involved had been promoted from the ranks. It is, in fact, largely due to the increasing resort to promotion from the executive and clerical classes (particularly under the stress of war and preparation for war in the period since 1938) that this social leaven has found its way into the higher ranks of the Service.

An examination of the social origins of new recruits to the administrative class by the open competitions of the five years 1949-53 helps us to judge what further changes in the same direction may be expected in the future.[1] Whereas only 9 per cent of the open competition entrants amongst our 1950 group were the children of manual workers, as many as 19 per cent of these recent recruits come into this category. In the 1950 group, a third of the open competition cases had fathers in either the church, medicine, law or teaching; amongst the open competition entrants of 1949-53 only a sixth were in this position. These changes are obviously important; comparison with the adult male population as a whole shows, however, that even the present-day direct entrants to the administrative class are by no means representative of society at large. Thus, whereas only some 3 per cent of adult males are in the Registrar-General's top social class category, 32 per cent of the fathers of these new recruits came from that status group. Category 2 —the intermediate occupations—has 15 per cent of all adult males, but 39 per cent of the fathers of new entrants. Category 3—skilled occupations (including ordinary clerks)—accounts for 52 per cent of adult males, but less than 26 per cent of the fathers. And categories 4 and 5 combined, in which 28 per cent of adult males are found, had only 3 per cent of the fathers.

These differences are still so large as to reflect major inequalities in the distribution of educational opportunity even in

[1] The 1953 competition figures, to which Sir Laurence Helsby refers on p. 42, are included in the present analysis.

the comparatively recent period when these new entrants were at school and university. We may hope, however, that when the full effects of the 1944 Education Act have made themselves felt, these discrepancies will be very much reduced. Recruitment policy has, of course, been substantially modified in a number of respects. First, it has been agreed that some 20 per cent of assistant principal vacancies should be filled by limited competition amongst those in the lower classes of the Service. Secondly, between 75 per cent and 50 per cent of new direct entrants are recruited on broadly the traditional lines, but with an interview of roughly three-quarters of an hour; it is much less likely that superficial qualities will get undue credit in a *viva voce* of this length than it was in the 15 minutes or so of pre-war practice. Thirdly, the remaining 25-50 per cent of direct entrants are being selected on the basis of the modified 'country house' procedure, where personality has greater weight than intellectual or academic ability. It is still too early to say whether those recruited by this new method differ significantly in their social origins from those chosen on the more traditional pattern; the limited data available so far suggest that they show a slightly greater tendency to come from the upper social strata.

Are the observed changes in the distribution of fathers' occupations, when the 1949-53 open competition entrants are compared with their pre-war counterparts, to be explained by the modifications that have taken place in the methods of selecting such entrants? The available evidence rather suggests that this is not so to any important extent. What appears to have happened is that there has been a marked alteration in the social background pattern of the universe of candidates presenting themselves for examination. The sample of successful candidates sieved out by the new selection methods is still apparently not a random one in terms of social origin, any more than it was before the war; but the change in the universe has naturally brought about consequential changes in the sample. The main hope of ultimately securing a more equal representation of those originating in the lower social strata must still lie in more widely dispersed educational opportunities, and in the maintenance and possible extension of the present more liberal policy of promotion from the ranks. It may well prove that one of the greatest difficulties will be that of ensuring that the groups of young people presenting themselves annually for competition are socially representative of those with the appropriate education and abilities. It was well known before the war, for instance, that the majority of successful candidates had been at either Oxford or Cambridge. This was to quite a large extent due to the fact that relatively few people who had not been at one or other of these two universities entered for the examination. Although, in the general field of post-war candidates, the other universities are better represented, most of them still contribute very much less than their appropriate share of competitors for entry to the administrative class. This under-representation itself contributes in some measure to the lack of social balance of the universe from which the sample of entrants has to be chosen. For though it is true, as Sir Laurence Helsby points out elsewhere in the present volume, that seven of the twelve working-class competition entrants of 1953 came from either Oxford or Cambridge, it is important to remember that these seven only formed 17 per cent of the Oxford and Cambridge contribution, whereas the remaining five cases of working-class origin formed no less than 45 per cent of the contribution from all other universities combined. The relative failure of the open competition to attract and select candidates from universities other than these two is still, therefore, tending to deprive the administrative class of recruits from the lower social strata.

Even when everything that can reasonably be expected has been done to encourage potential assistant principals from all walks of life to compete for entry, and even when greatly-improved opportunities for a secondary grammar and university education have had more time to affect the issue, there will still remain many factors contributing to an under-representation of those of lower-middle and working-class origin. The recent report of the Central Advisory Council for Education on early leaving has shown the extent to which grammar school children from these strata fail to justify the expectations arising from their performance at 11 +. Everyone is agreed that, quite apart from economic circumstances, the chances that appropriate numbers of such children will ever reach the requisite standard of formal education for direct entry to the administrative class are seriously weakened by the attitudes of parents, the example of friends, and by many other unfavourable environmental influences both inside and outside school and university. And for those in whose cases all these obstacles have been surmounted there still remain many additional adverse factors. The need to earn money as soon as possible, or make sure of a foothold in some profession, may be a deterrent to waiting even a few months and gambling on success in a highly competitive examination of the method I type; while method II may seem, with its emphasis on social rather than purely intellectual qualities, an unsatisfactory alternative. We can only hope that, as more reliable information becomes available regarding the nature of the process whereby, at all stages from early childhood onwards, potential entrants to this and other professions are weeded out, social policy will be so adapted as to ensure a greater flow of recruits from the largest reservoir of talent, the families of the lower-middle and working classes.

Chapter 13

THE CIVIL SERVICE IN FRANCE

By P. CHATENET

(*Director of the French Civil Service*)

THIS brief study does not aim at a full description of French administration nor even at an exposition of the fundamental rules according to which it is governed. It seeks, more simply, to outline and explain its original features, particularly when it is compared to Anglo-Saxon administrative institutions.

These original features, we must first note, are much less the result of legal and logical constructions set up *a priori* than of concepts which stem from a long historical tradition. At least this was true until the great Imperial reforms of the first years of the nineteenth century. Up to that time, there had been few great administrative reformers in France, or, rather, the great reforms that had taken place had only regulated or modified institutions which were the product of a long historical evolution.

The essential attributes of the French administrative system, i.e. those fundamental characteristics which are original to it, are derived from the close connection between administration and the political sovereign over the centuries. The stability and the continuity of the administrative system have thus led to the survival within administrative life of principles belonging to vanished political systems.

It should not be thought, however, that French administration has remained static over the centuries; new ideas and social forces have superimposed new concepts upon earlier principles; these new concepts have not destroyed the ancient structure; but they have radically modified its character.

1. *The Superiority of the State*

France is a country of Roman and statute law. It is therefore no matter for surprise that one of the fundamental principles regulating its institutions should be that of the supremacy of law, i.e. of the written statute. Furthermore, the notion of democracy in France expresses itself essentially in the sovereignty of the people; and the will of the people, considered as the source of all sovereignty, of all *imperium*, finds expression in the law, voted by the representatives of the people. As a consequence, there exists a fundamental inequality between the administration and the '*administrés*'. For French administration rests upon the authority of the state and that authority pervades simultaneously the relations of the administration with private individuals and the internal structure of the administration itself.

The origin of this concept, as of French law as a whole, must be sought in the juridical institutions of ancient Rome, and more particularly in the notion of *potestas*. The first jurists of the French monarchy succeeded in combining the heritage of Roman law with Christian principles and they elaborated a theory of power, that of divine right, which was to serve as the foundation for the political and administrative system of absolute monarchy.

Owing to the intellectual movement of the eighteenth century and to the political events of the French Revolution of 1789, the basis of power changed. The People replaced God. But the principles remained, especially that of the inequality between the administration and the private citizen. As a result, there exists in France what might be called a juridical dualism: there is the right of the individual which forms private law and the right of the state which is public law. The latter is autonomous and has its own rules and jurisdiction.

In regard to the Civil Service, with which we are more particularly concerned here, the consequence of this has been that, from the earliest times until the present day, the relations between the state and its agents have been different from the common law relations between employers and employees. Since the administration is organized according to a principle of authority, its relations with its agents cannot be founded on equality. Therefore, they cannot be determined by contractual arrangements. It is customary to express this concept by saying that, in France, the civil servant is in a *situation réglementaire*, which means that the various aspects of his employment are not determined as in the case of a contract for ordinary work, but are decided unilaterally by the state in its rôle of political sovereign.

To this notion of inequality, there has been added another

162

basic principal of the juridical and administrative evolution of France; this is the tendency to centralization.

2. *The Centralizing Spirit*

The propensity to centralization was a natural consequence of absolute power based on divine right. The taste for logic and for a unified system applicable to everyone over the whole country, which could already be found among the great administrators of the absolute monarchy, reached its full climax in the Revolution, the Consulate and the Empire. French governments have always lived in fear of federalism—it is in the name of the unity of the Republic that the Jacobins sent the Girondins to the guillotine during the Revolution—and it is this fear which explains, in particular, why local government in France has never reached the development which it achieved in the Anglo-Saxon or Germanic systems.

This centralizing spirit has also affected the Civil Service. In this connection, the most remarkable period in French history is that of the Consulate and the Empire and, though a hundred and fifty years have passed (during more than half of which liberal democracy prevailed), the principles which were then applied have continued to dominate French administrative organization.

As a result, there has occurred throughout the nineteenth century a multiplication of general rules applicable to the whole of the Civil Service. The reason why these rules were not codified is that the idea of a status for the Civil Service appeared for a long time as contrary to the notion of the state's prerogative of unilateral decision to which reference has already been made. Nevertheless, the most important regulations affecting civil servants were slowly unified. The *Conseil d'État* played a vital rôle in this process of unification because of its jurisdiction in administrative disputes, which was of crucial importance in the elaboration of the regulations affecting the Civil Service.

Legislation forming a general code for the Civil Service was only passed in 1946 and it is important to see that the delay was a consequence of the principle of authority, not of a taste for diversity; indeed, the legislation of 1946 was in a sense a codification of general rules stemming from practice or jurisprudence.

One example will help to show the propensity to centralization in regard to the Civil Service. Colonial civil servants, despite the difference of their position, are practically subject to the same rules as their colleagues in metropolitan France.

3. *Permanence*

Another feature very soon appeared in the administrative evolution of France: the concern with permanence.

French administration has always known a high degree of permanence in its personnel. One can say that nothing like the spoils system has ever existed in France. Under the Monarchy, the relative lack of permanence of the *commissaires* was counterbalanced by the permanence of *officiers*, who owned their offices.

The civil servant has almost never appeared bound to a government, still less to a party—he is the servant of the state, which like him is permanent. This is at once a consequence of French juridical dualism and of our taste for abstraction. The idea of permanence is accepted by public opinion and it is solidly anchored in the minds of civil servants, who long had a nostalgia for the venality of offices. Venality was re-established for certain posts under the Bourbon restoration; the Gouvion Saint-Cyr legislation gave to military officers a kind of ownership of their rank.

In practice, however, the French Civil Service has known very few 'purges' and these have always, or almost always, been followed by a reaction in the direction of stability. The half-pay system for the officers of Napoleon under the *Restauration* contributed to the passage of legislation on the status of officers. The system of dossiers of General André, which was a consequence of the storms caused in the army by the Dreyfus affair, led to the passing of the law of 1905 on the communication of his dossier to the civil servant, which is one of the civil servant's essential guarantees, since it compels the administration to acquaint him very fully with the charges laid against him before he is subjected to a disciplinary measure.

An examination of Civil Service lists reveals that from 1847 to 1852—i.e. within five years which witnessed four different régimes—the July Monarchy, the democratic Republic, the conservative Republic and the Second Empire—the changes in higher and middle-grade personnel (with the exception of Prefects) hardly exceeded those that would have been caused by retirement, resignation, or death in a period of political stability. The same is true for the period 1869-74, the years of transition from the Second Empire to the Third Republic.

This stability in practice has slowly been institutionalized; statutes created a body of law where there had only been long practice and the notion of stability itself changed. Permanence, which had primarily been viewed as a means of ensuring the necessary stability to the state, became a means of protecting the interests of the state's agents; this evolution, which accorded with civil servants' deep-rooted wishes, served to bring into sharp focus the idea of 'guarantees'; it also helped to limit the state's authority and to increase the unification of the service.

It is essential clearly to grasp this fundamental transformation in order to understand how it was possible for a system of guarantees, which makes the French civil servant one of the best protected citizens against the arbitrary power of the state, to grow out of an administrative régime originally based on the principles of authority and inequality.

4. *The Development of Guarantees*

Recent changes have increased the individual rights of civil servants *vis-à-vis* the state; but these changes have not destroyed earlier principles. The law of 19th October 1946, which defines the status of civil servants, lays down in Article 5 that '*le fonctionnaire est vis-à-vis de l'administration dans une situation statutaire et réglementaire*', which is in accordance with the best classical doctrine. In practice, however, the emergence of codified rules limits the state's ability to make use of those powers it continues to enjoy. The power remains, but its exercise is determined, directed and sometimes prevented by a whole system of preliminary consultations and subsequent appeals which provide civil servants with a tight mesh of guarantees. This compromise between the authority of the administration and the protection of the civil servants' interests was achieved as a result of a variety of factors, the most important of which was the development of trade unionism.

For a long time, both the political rulers and administrative jurisprudence viewed with suspicion any association of civil servants and, when the trade union legislation of 1884 was passed, it was explicitly laid down that civil servants would remain outside its scope. Some years later, in 1901, legislation gave to every citizen the right of association. Could civil servants be as rigorously prevented from joining associations as they had been prevented from forming unions? The governments of the period did not think so and—by making a distinction which must appear rather surprising to the layman—civil servants were granted the right of forming associations while the right to belong to a trade union was still denied them. The reason for this, which is quite peculiar to French law, is explained by the fear of seeing civil servants ally themselves to ordinary wage-earners within a trade union movement which paraded revolutionary tendencies and believed in the general strike as its essential weapon.

This hostility to the development of trade unionism in the Civil Service has faded as a result of political evolution and also because of the new orientation of the unions, which have become less concerned with political revolution than with the defence of professional interests. Immediately after the first world war, unions of civil servants were formed and, although they were not recognized, they were at least tolerated. Experience was to show that it was entirely unrealistic to cling to a legalistic distinction between associations and trade unions and that, if one must negotiate with representatives of civil servants, it was better to do so with representative union delegates than with members of associations enjoying no support among civil servants. The legislation of 1946 acknowledges the full union rights of civil servants.

In the event, the participation of union representatives in administrative life has not led to the revolutionary upheaval which was feared by the governments of the end of the nineteenth century. Union delegates have shown themselves more inclined to foster the growth of guarantees, calculated to consolidate acquired advantages, than to seek the destruction of the existing system.

Civil Service unionism in France has thus made a powerful contribution to the struggle against arbitrariness which had been initiated by the *Conseil d'État*, and it has also helped the growth of consultative bodies intended to counterbalance the omnipotence of the state.

In its present form, the French Civil Service, minutely regulated by the legislation of 1946, presents some original features, the nature of which may warrant fairly detailed description. We shall select three examples, those of recruitment, promotion, and discipline.

(*a*) Appointments are made by the relevant administrative authorities but this does not mean that their choice is free. Both in order to ensure high-level entrants and to prevent any kind of favouritism, most appointments are made after a competitive examination. The administrative authorities have, it is true, the power to draw up the list of candidates eligible to compete, but, in accordance with democratic principles, the government exercises its discretionary power in this matter under the strict judicial control of the *Conseil d'État* and under the political control of parliament. In addition, the examining board entrusted with the task of appraising the examination results is possessed of a very high degree of independence and appointments must be made in the order of the list which the board draws up. In this way while the power of appointment continues in principle to belong to the administrative authorities, that power is in practice considerably limited by the examination system.

(*b*) Promotion is the result of a selection made by the administrative authorities and that selection was for a long time a matter of discretion. The desire to avoid promotions on the basis of favouritism and the pressure of the unions to have all civil servants guaranteed a normal career have led to the elaboration of rules of promotion. With the exception of some higher posts, promotions can only be made according to a well-defined procedure. This procedure first narrows down the number of those eligible for promotion by laying down the conditions of seniority required for eligibility. The rules then require that a promotion list be made up in which are included the eligible candidates in order of merit. The list is made up by the administrative authorities, but only after the advisory opinion of a commission which includes an equal number of representatives of the administration and of the personnel has been received. Promotions must be made according to the order of the list.

(*c*) Disciplinary measures are promulgated by the relevant administrative authority but the civil servant is protected against arbitrary sanctions by preliminary guarantees and by the possibility of appeal after the sanction has been promulgated.

Before any sanction can be applied, the authority is compelled to communicate his dossier to the civil servant so as to allow him to present his defence; he must therefore be fully informed of the charges laid against him. If the proposed sanction is of a serious nature, the administrative authority must summon a board of discipline which includes representatives of the personnel; the civil servant may present his defence before this board and he may be assisted by counsel.

Once it has received the advice of the board, the administrative authority freely makes its decision; if, however, it decides upon a sanction more serious than that proposed by the board of discipline, the civil servant has the right of appeal either to the *Conseil Supérieur de la Fonction Publique* or to the relevant administrative tribunals.

It may be seen from this brief survey that the decision of the administrative authority is never tied to the advice which the authority is compelled to seek; in practice, however, the desire to maintain good working relations with the personnel induces the authority to consider very carefully the recommendations made by the consultative bodies. Where the authority is strong enough to accept the advice given in certain cases and to reject it in others in the best interests of the Service, the system which was installed in 1946 allows a fairly harmonious balance to be struck between the prerogatives of the state and the legitimate interests of civil servants. Where, on the other hand, the authority is weak, the system entails the risk of allowing too large a scope to professional interests to the detriment of the general interest for which the government alone is responsible. There must always remain an irreducible minimum of discretion without which any kind of administration becomes impossible.

Those aspects of administrative organization and more particularly of the French Civil Service which have been examined here, lead one to wonder whether the problem of the relations of the Civil Service to the government exists under the same conditions in France as in England. What we most readily admire in the British Civil Service is its remarkable capacity of forming a corporate body without for all that behaving like an autonomous power in the state. This is one of the most delicate problems of democracy. For democracy presupposes that political rulers will change in accordance with the shifts of opinion of the majority of the sovereign people. In contradistinction, the continuous functioning of public services and their ever-increasing technicality require a certain permanence of the civil servants who run them. Is there a danger that this need for permanence might induce in civil servants a tendency to independence in relation to the political rulers and that this tendency might lead them to constitute a true administrative power within the state?

In England, the experience of a hundred years has demonstrated the accuracy of Sir Charles Trevelyan's vision, since the servants of the Crown have been able to find in their loyalty to the Crown the basis of a permanence which they have succeeded in reconciling with respect for the political changes inherent in a democracy.

In France, the taste for logic and the tradition of statute law have resulted in an appeal to a more abstract notion, that of the state. Yet, it may well be asked if this notion of the state is really so abstract. For it was begotten by the jurists of the Capetian kings, imposed by the strong will of the absolute monarchs, fused with the idea of nationhood by the Jacobins, codified by Napoleon I and humanized by liberal democracy, so that the continuity of the state is identified in France with the history of the French people. As a result, it legitimately serves as a foundation for the search by civil servants of the necessary conciliation between a rigorous respect for the permanent interests of the nation and a loyal obedience to those whom the rules of democracy appoint to lead it.

Chapter 14

THE RECRUITMENT AND TRAINING OF HIGHER CIVIL SERVANTS IN THE UNITED KINGDOM AND FRANCE

By ANDRÉ BERTRAND
(*Professor of Law; Director of Studies,
École Nationale d'Administration, Paris*)

IN his recent book, 'Constitutional Government and Democracy', Professor Carl Friedrich called bureaucracy 'the core of modern government'. This statement is indisputably true as regards both Great Britain and France. Our two countries, today, are to a great extent—irrespective of the political party or parties in power—welfare states. In order to fulfill its ever growing tasks, many of them new and very technical, especially in the economic and social fields, the Executive must be able to rely on a body of permanent civil servants equipped with a broad and sound education, properly selected, well trained and adapted to their important and difficult jobs.

Great Britain and France have been well aware of this need for a long time. In the two countries, during the second half of the nineteenth century, the necessity was felt for a merit system based on open competitive examination, in order to supersede patronage or its French equivalent: *le libre choix du Ministre*. Parallel to the setting up of the Civil Service Commission in 1855 and the introduction in 1870 of organized competitive examinations in Britain was the holding in France, as early as 1847 and 1849, of the first competitive examinations to recruit for the *Inspection générale des finances*, and the *Conseil d'État*. The same process became generally enforced in the various *administrations centrales* between 1870 and 1890, from the beginning of the Third Republic.[1]

---

[1] One ought to recall also the short-lived experience of the École d'Administration set up in 1848 by the provisional government of the Second Republic. Admission to it was based on an open competitive exam-

170

From the start, the English system aimed at fighting against excessive departmentalism. It tended towards unification and centralization. A single, permanent body, the Civil Service Commission, conducted all the examinations for the whole Civil Service. Quite logically, within the framework of the Executive and the structure of the Civil Service, such a system led to the creation of the establishment branch of the Treasury in 1919; and, after a long evolution, to the building up of a unified administrative class in 1920 (although the Foreign Office was kept apart and remains so, even after the 1943 reforms).

For a long time, the situation in France was altogether different. Up to 1945, the recruitment of the young civil servants, at the same level, remained the responsibility of each *Grand Corps* (*Conseil d'État, Cour des Comptes, Ministère des Affaires Étrangères, Inspection Générale des Finances*) and of each department. The defects of such an organization were obvious. The programmes of the various competitive examinations were too narrowly specialized, in close relation with the tasks of the *Grands Corps* or department concerned. The jury of each examination being composed only, or nearly completely, of members of the recruiting *Grands Corps* or department, a spirit of co-optation was bound to develop. Besides, all this did not help to arouse a feeling of unity amongst the civil servants of the various branches of the Executive, nor did it make it possible to give the French Civil Service a unified structure.

It was only after the second world war, in an atmosphere favourable to profound changes and after a thorough study of the English system, taken in many respects as an example to be followed, that a drastic decision was reached in October 1945. All individual examinations of the *Grands Corps* and departments were suppressed and one new one was set up, opening the door to a National School of Administration which was then established and about which more will be said later. Simultaneously, a *Direction de la fonction publique* was created under the Prime Minister's authority and a year later the Act of 19th October

ination. But it was suppressed in 1849, owing to the dual opposition of the Ministers (who did not want to lose their freedom of choosing the newcomers to the Civil Service), and of the University and, more particularly, of the Faculties of Law, which feared that some of the best students would rather go to the School than to them.

1946 laid down a body of rules common to all civil servants and, more particularly, a general statute for civil servants of the administrative class.

A similar evolution can also be observed in both countries as regards the social origin of the higher Civil Service. In 1854, Trevelyan and Northcote, in their famous report, took it for granted that the candidates ought to be 'the youth of the upper and middle classes'. And so they actually were for many years.

In the same way, in France, after the foundation in 1871 (twenty-four years before the London School of Economics and Political Science) of the *École libre des Sciences Politiques*, which was quickly to acquire a *de facto* monopoly in the training of the candidates for the *Grands Corps* examinations, all or most of them at least belonged to the upper and middle bourgeoisie and —France being an overcentralized country—nearly always to the Parisian bourgeoisie. The situation was slightly different, however, as regards the *rédactorats*, the examinations leading to the various departments of the government, to which was attached less prestige and for which a fair proportion of candidates were of more humble origin, sons, for instance, of lower civil servants, who had read law in Paris or in a provincial university.

Nevertheless, after the first world war, the governments began to realize that, in a true democracy, the Civil Service must be a comprehensively representative cross-section of the whole community, its members being drawn from all elements of the nation, rich or poor. In England, a very broad scheme of scholarships to Oxford and Cambridge was begun and thanks to it and because most of the successful candidates to the Civil Service Commission examinations were graduates from these two universities, the administrative class became more democratic in its recruitment.

In France, where, in a way, the problem was less acute, as university studies were, and are still, much cheaper, the *École libre des Sciences Politiques*, a more expensive college as it was private, began also on a smaller scale, in the thirties, to grant scholarships eagerly fought for by French students whose families' means were very limited.

But this new trend became much more powerful after the second world war and took on a different shape. The new idea was not only to give a chance to all brilliant university students, irrespective of the social class to which they belonged, but also to secure the promotion of those who had not been able to go to the university at all and who had entered the Civil Service younger and at a lower level. Thus appeared in Great Britain the limited competition reserved to civil servants of the executive class and destined to fill 20% of the vacancies in the administrative class.

In France, when the National School of Administration was set up, in October 1945, a drastic measure was adopted. It was decided that two parallel entrance examinations to the School would be organized: the first (commonly called the *concours-étudiants*) was opened only to graduates of the universities, but the second (commonly referred to as the *concours fonctionnaires*) was reserved for all those who had already served the state, in any capacity, for at least five years, no university degree being necessary for these candidates. From the beginning, the total number of vacancies to be filled each year was equally divided between the two examinations.

These reforms have now been in force for nearly ten years and the sociological inquiries which have recently been carried out by Mr Bottomore and Mr Kelsall tend to show that, in fact, this democratization process has gone further in Great Britain than in France.[1] But in both countries, the new direction taken is clear and will certainly produce more important results in the near future.[2]

So far, therefore, the parallel drawn between our two countries reveals more elements of similarity than of opposition. In both cases, we find a tendency towards a unified and increasingly democratic organization of recruitment.

But the picture changes, if we consider two other more technical problems:

[1] See T. B. Bottomore, 'La mobilité sociale dans la haute administration française' in *Cahiers Internationaux de Sociologie*, Vol. XIII, 1952, and 'Higher Civil Servants in France' in *Transactions of the Second World Congress of Sociology*, Vol. II, 1954; R. K. Kelsall, *Higher Civil Servants in Britain*, London, 1955, and chapter 12 of the present book, 'The Social Background of the Higher Civil Service'.

[2] The latest entrance examinations to the National School of Administration for the years 1952-54 inclusive seem to bear out this remark. They reveal an increasing proportion of candidates coming from the poorer classes of society.

(1) What criteria of aptitude are chosen, in order to get the best possible men in the higher Civil Service?

(2) What kind of professional training is needed by the young civil servants, once they have been selected? Will it be purely empirical and acquired within the Civil Service itself or will it be organic, exterior, so to speak, to the Civil Service and entrusted to a school? In short, this second problem consists in the discussion of the usefulness of a national school of administration. We shall now concentrate on these two questions.

*   *   *

In Great Britain, to quote Macaulay's own words, the recruitment ought to be based on 'a liberal education'. Macaulay's view still prevails today. The best graduates in any subject—be it Greek, botany or mathematics—will eventually, it is held, make the best civil servants.

In France, with the tradition of the *légistes* of the ancient régime and in a country of written law, candidates for the administrative posts of the Civil Service, were required to undergo an academic education in the faculty of law. (It should however, be pointed out, that law is taught in France as a subject of general culture and not in a professional way, and that the syllabi in the French faculties of law include courses in economics.) Except for the examination of the Ministry of Foreign Affairs and a few others, a law degree was a compulsory requirement.

Again one must emphasize the part played by the *École libre des Sciences Politiques* in the training of the candidates for the *Grands Corps de l'État*. The teaching there dealt in a much broader sense with the social sciences, and not, except for a relatively few courses, with legal technicalities. Practically all the members of the *Grands Corps* had therefore enjoyed this wider education before entering the Service. But such was not necessarily the case with the candidates for the various departmental examinations, and the programmes of all the examinations, including those for the *Grands Corps*, were closely connected with those of the law degrees.

Now the present rôle of the higher Civil Service in a welfare state—to help and advise the executive in determining policies, to carry them out when the executive has, under the control of

Parliament, made its decision about them—is of the widest nature. For the civil servant, law is an instrument, a useful one, even in certain respects an indispensable one,[1] but political science, economics, demography, sociology, social psychology, etc., can alone provide the fundamental elements of knowledge on which public policies are to be founded. Therefore, when, in 1945, the entrance examinations to the *École Nationale d'Administration* were organized, a new balance had to be struck. Breaking away from the old rule, it was decided, for the first examination, that the *licence en droit* would no longer be compulsory. Any other *licence* in arts, sciences, etc. was deemed sufficient. This was, no doubt, an important move in the British direction.

But, even so, the specific criteria of aptitude which are adopted today in Great Britain and in France still vary to a large extent, from two different points of view: first, as regards the subject matter of examinations and secondly, the methods devised to find out, not only the intellectual qualities of the candidates, but their true value as men and future responsible officials of the state.

The higher civil servant might be described as 'the social scientist in action'. The programmes of the French entrance examinations to the *École Nationale d'Administration*, if they do not completely match this definition, are fairly closely connected with it. All the candidates must write the following papers:

(1) An essay on a subject dealing with the general evolution of political, economic and social ideas and facts since the middle of the eighteenth century; that is, a paper founded on *la culture générale* in its widest sense;

(2) An essay on the political institutions of the principal contemporary states or on the fundamentals of French administrative law;

(3) An essay on economic policies;

(4) A translation into French of a text written in a foreign language (for the students' examination) or a summary of a longer text or a group of several texts (for the civil servants' examination).

---

[1] It must be recalled that every high civil servant, in France, must be able to draft bills and regulatory texts, in legal technical terms, before they are examined by the *Conseil d'État*. The French administration does not rely on a body of experts such as the English parliamentary draftsmen.

Those of the candidates who have been declared admissible have one more paper to write. This paper deals with administrative law, financial science and legislation, social economy or the history of international relations, according to the section of the School they wish to enter.[1]

It is clear that the education received either in the faculty of law or in the faculty of arts or in the Institute of Political Studies[2] will, as a rule, be insufficient by itself to enable a candidate to master all the subjects of such papers. In fact, the average successful candidate must have attended at least two of the three institutions. And the statistics of the students' examinations reveal that about two-thirds of the *reçus* have graduated from both the faculty of law and the Institute of Political Studies.[3] We consider this to be a satisfactory result.

It would be futile in this brief chapter to attempt to analyse in detail the various papers comprising the English examination (method I). Compared with the French, they reveal a very striking contrast and they show how much the English approach to the same problem remains different from the French. I would make only a few comments on this point.

Taken as a whole, the various compulsory papers in Britain— essay, English, Present Day—are devised to test the more general aptitudes of the candidates, their capability to grasp non-specialized subjects, their power of expression and faculty of judgment. They cannot—and obviously are not intended to— prove if these candidates possess the basic knowledge of problems with which a modern administration is confronted every day.

One would nevertheless be ready to approve fully of the

[1] There are four sections within the School: General Administration, Economic and Financial Administration, Social Administration, and External Affairs.

[2] In October 1945, when the École Nationale d'Administration was set up, the *École libre des Sciences Politiques* was nationalized and became the Institute of Political Studies of the University of Paris. At the same date and in the following years, similar Institutes of Political Studies, as a measure of cultural decentralization, were created at the universities of Strasbourg, Lyons, Grenoble, Bordeaux, Toulouse and Algiers.

[3] Supplementary marks can be allotted to candidates who volunteer to pass *viva voce* on scientific subjects, being graduates of the faculty of sciences or holding the diploma of a scientific *Grande École* such as *l'École Polytechnique*. This provision is not made frequent use of by the candidates; in other words, few of them hold such degrees or diplomas.

system, if such papers were counterbalanced by others, aimed at checking this basic knowledge; but far from it! Amongst the hundred or so optional subjects,[1] the highest marks are allotted to the subjects included in the mathematics and science groups, the lowest to these comprising the law, philosophy, politics and economics group. (Incidentally, it is surprising not to find sociology mentioned here.) There is something of a paradox, for a French mind, in such a distribution of the marks. I must confess that I do not believe that very high marks in higher botany, geology or zoology are truly indicative of the candidate's aptitude to become a brilliant civil servant in the Treasury, the Board of Trade or the Ministry of Labour. It appears, actually, that in spite of the 'premium' so offered to scientific subjects, the great majority of the candidates do not take them. But the fact remains that they can be successful without having their knowledge of any of the various social sciences tested.

From this first point of view, the French régime seems to me better adapted to the true needs of the modern state. But, on the contrary, the British way of testing the candidate *as a whole*, of trying to find out the man and not only his intellectual brilliance, deserves, in my opinion, the highest praise and the French approach to the problem has remained, thus far, more timid.

It must be remembered, though, that traditionally French examinations have always been partly based on a *viva voce* test. It was so, before 1945, for the numerous individual examinations of the *Grands Corps* and departments. It is still true of the entrance examinations to the *École Nationale d'Administration*. There are two *viva voce* at the student's examination, and one at the civil servants'.[2] And even if these *viva voce*, like the written papers, deal with precise subjects and are therefore intellectual tests of knowledge, through the direct contact they

[1] Incidentally, this very vast number of optional subjects must lead to a purely technical, but practically important difficulty: that of equalizing or standardizing the marks granted by so many different examiners.

[2] The subject matter of these *viva voce* vary, according to the section of the School the candidates wish to enter. For instance, in the section of Financial and Economic Administration, at the students' examination, the two *viva voce* deal with social economics and human and economic geography.

establish between the examiner and the candidate they are bound to become, up to a point, a test of alertness, common sense, power of reasoning, etc.

Furthermore, and after the British model, the French have adopted, since 1945, the test of the interview, in a modified way, so as to fit in with French habits. The interview is called—to quote the regulations about it—'a conversation of twenty minutes with the jury, the starting point being the commentary in ten minutes of a text of a general character.' But, in practice, this conversation remains far removed from the English interview. It was felt in France, when this new test was set up, that the conversation had to be started by 'something'. Hence, the commentary that precedes it. But this commentary is a fairly intellectual process and, more often than not, at least half of the twenty minutes are spent by the candidate answering questions about the text itself, its meaning, its author, etc. One ought to add, however, that the jury certainly takes into account, not only the answers themselves, but also, and perhaps more, what they may reveal, as regards the candidates' faculty of judgment, strength of character, and other qualities on the whole. I feel that this test, although it represents a very considerable improvement of our previous system, is still far from yielding as rich and diversified information about the candidates as its English counterpart.

And, of course, by 'its English counterpart', I mean not only the interview before the F.I.B. (method I), but still more the series of tests and interviews at the C.S.S.B. and the decisive interview before the F.S.B., as they are conducted in the open competition (method II) and in the limited competition. It seems indeed difficult to imagine a more comprehensive scheme of discovering the all-round qualities of the candidates.

One must probably admit, however, that it is fairly difficult, with method II, *objectively* to establish the final order of merit amongst the candidates—or, rather, to convince easily every one concerned that it has been so established. Probably this objection will always prevent the French government from adopting a similar system. And it is certainly a remarkable proof of the unlimited confidence bestowed upon the Civil Service Commissioners that method II, as it is organized, can function in Great Britain without complaints. Anyway, handled as it is, by able and impartial people, it is a device that ought to bring excellent results.

I believe, therefore, and hope that, at the end of the experimental period, after 1957, method II will continue operating and will perhaps apply to a greater proportion of the vacancies to be filled by open competition. But it remains a fact that, even after going through these tests, either of the British or of the French type—or, indeed, of any conceivable type—the successful candidates have still, professionally speaking, to learn their job. How are they, then, to learn it?

*   *   *

It is on this point that the comparison of our two systems is of the utmost interest. At the start, and up to 1945, the situation was roughly the same in both countries. The young civil servant of the administrative class, immediately after passing his entrance examination, began, quite empirically and in the most haphazard way, to learn his job and its technicalities *on the spot*. Nothing, it was argued, could replace a personal and practical experience of the tasks to be performed. As the French saying goes, *c'est en forgeant qu'on devient forgeron*.

Such a conception was perhaps in harmony with the liberal state of the nineteenth century, the law and order state whose attributions were fairly limited.

Today, taking into consideration the machinery of the entrance examinations, this practice could be more easily admitted in France, where most of the basic knowledge of the candidates in the field of social sciences has been, as it has been shown, carefully scrutinized through various papers and *viva voce*. But in spite of this, it is in France, and not in Great Britain, that a civil servants' training school was set up in 1945. A fact which, incidentally, reveals that the French 1945 reforms, as regards the Civil Service, have been, so to speak, the blending of an English notion—a unified Civil Service—and of a typically French idea, that of a *Grande École*, so dear to the French hearts since the Revolution (example, *l'École Polytechnique*, set up by the Convention).

In Great Britain, although a similar measure has been advocated since 1944 (in particular, by the Assheton Committee), no such school or college has been as yet set up. One finds only a departmental training of a very limited character, which varies to a great extent from one department to another, and, apart from it, very remarkable, but quite short, intensive courses run by the Treasury.[1]

In France, on the contrary, since 1945, all of our young civil servants of the same class pass through *l'École Nationale d'Administration* where they have thorough professional training extending over nearly three years. The first year, which they pass away from Paris, consists entirely of a *stage*, under the guidance of a *préfet* in the *départements* or of various administrators and *contrôleurs civils* in Algeria, Morocco or Tunisia: that is to say, in all cases, of high civil servants in positions of responsibility, who are not specialized, except in general administration of every possible kind. The young civil servant is in close contact with his chief and his most intimate collaborators, while becoming acquainted with the various state services one finds in a *préfecture*, a *commune mixte* of Algeria, or an administrative district in Morocco or Tunisia. The objectives of such *stages* are manifold. Humanly, they aim at developing the character and personality of the *stagiaires*. Intellectually, they give them a wide insight into all sorts of administrative problems. More technically, they allow them to see how administrative affairs are actually handled in concrete cases, to understand local needs and the way they can be met on the spot (not by red tape or central action), and to discover the methods and procedures of administration. One might say that the *stage* is, in a way, the French equivalent, expanded over the period of a year, of the English method II. When it is over, the head of the *stagiaire* sends the school a written opinion of the *stagiaire*, which takes into account the main elements of his personality (from physical vigour and aptitude for work, to moral and psychological gifts, including intellectual qualities and strength of character). On the basis of this opinion and of his own judgment, the *Directeur des Stages* awards a mark to each *stagiaire* concerned, which can be regarded as the

---

[1] For the last three or four years, one or two French civil servants, engaged in their first or third and last year of training at the *École Nationale d'Administration*, have taken part in these courses, by the kind permission of the Treasury. They have been extremely interested in the work done in Whitehall

numerical expression of the all-round judgment passed on him.

By the end of the first year, the *stagiaires* are also requested to write a *mémoire de stage*, in the form of a twenty-five to thirty page essay on a particular problem that they happened to have come across and become interested in during their *stage*, and about which they must make personal, concrete, constructive remarks and suggestions for reform. A special jury marks each *mémoire* after having, if necessary, demanded further explanations from its author.

After their *stage*, the civil servants come back to Paris and spend the second year at the School itself, following a cycle of studies of a systematic and more intellectual character. By means of these studies, the civil servants are able to broaden, deepen and systematize, in an administrative approach, various elements of knowledge that they had previously acquired and, in many cases, applied in actual administrative life during the preceding year. At the same time, they receive a professional training designed to develop sound and efficient working methods: the impulse toward objectivity, the aptitude to analyse first, and then to synthesize, common sense and the power to judge and to reason, the ability to find out positive and practical solutions to various administrative problems, etc.

The keystone of the system, during this second year, is the *travaux des conférences*, for the organization of which the probationers are divided into small groups of ten to fifteen which meet regularly three times a week, all the year round, for two hours each time. These *travaux des conférences* are conducted by civil servants between 30 and 40 years of age, belonging to the *Grands Corps* or to the main departments of the executive or, in a few cases, by professors of law or economics. Some of them are common to all the civil servants, but the majority are followed by the students of a given section and their subject-matter varies according to the section concerned.[1] All are based on *exposés* (delivered by the civil servants and criticized by their comrades and finally by their tutors), on general discussions, or sometimes on studies of particular questions carried out by hypothetical interdepartmental committees, the members of which are each

---

[1] For instance, in the section of economic and financial administration, two series of *travaux de conférence* deal respectively with economic and financial matters, and with business organization and management.

supposed to represent a certain department. In addition, the probationers have to write various papers during the year, half of which take the form of administrative documents such as reports to a high official, *exposés des motifs* of a bill, circular letters of instruction to external services, etc. All the papers are corrected by the *maîtres de conférences* and given marks. It is clear that, with all these tests, each probationer can be individually judged very throughly by his *maîtres de conférences*, so that, by the end of the second year, each can be awarded a synthetic mark (*note d'exercices*) by the *Directeur des Études* whose task is of an equalizing or standardizing nature, based on the *maîtres des conférences'* proposals and in agreement with them.

Apart from the *travaux des conférences*, some lectures, dealing with the problems that confront a modern welfare state, are delivered by university professors or, more frequently, by high civil servants. Foreign languages are taught; physical training and individual sports and team games must also be indulged in once a week.

All the probationers then go through a classification examination consisting of three papers, two *viva voce* (two of the tests being common to all of them, while three bear on programmes which vary according to the section to which the pupils belong) and one test in a foreign language (or two in two different ones for the pupils of the external affairs section).

An order of merit is then established, according to the first year marks (10), the second year marks (10) and the classification examination marks (30) and the probationers are asked, in the order of their rank (from the top to the bottom of the list), to choose one of the careers for which their section has prepared them.[1]

The third and last year then begins. It starts with a second *stage*, but of a very different kind. It lasts for about two months

[1] Some of the careers are common to all sections (*Conseil d'État, Contrôles civils du Maroc et de Tunisie*) or to the three first sections (*Cour des Comptes, Inspection des Finances*); others are 'divided' between 2 or 3 sections (*Ministère de l'Interieur, Corps de l'expansion économique a l'étranger*); most of them are reserved to one specific section (for instance the *Ministère des Finances* to the section of economic and financial administration, the *Ministère des Affaires Etrangères* to the section of external affairs, etc.). In fact, the first on the list choose, as a rule, positions offered in the *Grands Corps*.

in a private firm, such as an industrial or commercial company or a bank. It is felt that the modern civil servant must be acquainted with the employers' responsibilities, organization and methods of work, with the problems of their employee relations, trade unions and so on. Once more, the probationer's experience is broadened in new domains which may be of the utmost interest for him, especially if he is to serve in an economic or financial corps or department. Furthermore, one can assume that these *stages*, by helping civil servants and business men to know each other better, will tend to bridge the gap between the public and the private sectors. Private firms have been quite co-operative in building up the *stages* and the probationers enjoy them very much.

When this new experience is over, the civil servants return for the last time to the School for three or four months. In place of the four sections previously used, seven or eight more specialized divisions are created, corresponding to the corps or department to which the probationers are already appointed. Within each of these divisions, practical work is carried out, on the basis of the case-method. The *directeurs des travaux pratiques* make their pupils study actual files taken out of their offices, in order to train them to handle the kind of affairs they will be in charge of after leaving the School. During the same period, the probationers spend part of their time in their corps or department, so that they become quite familiar with the machinery of government as a whole and with the internal structure of their own organ of administration in particular. These concluding studies are a last phase of transition at the end of which they begin their lives as active civil servants.

Such is the system which, since 1945, has turned out more than 600 high civil servants in France. It is a fairly long process, one must admit. But the time which seems so freely granted to the School may appear in the long run to be saved by the state, because there is no need, after the School, of any in-service training, necessary in other countries, but always disruptive of normal administrative work. Is there a danger, on the other hand, since all civil servants are bound to go through one school, of creating a monolithic Civil Service—a danger of bias and indoctrination? It does not seem so, if one considers the extreme diversity of opinions, origins and positions amongst the School's professors, *maîtres de conférences* and *directeures de travaux pratiques;* and, furthermore, the equally extreme diversity and the average age (about 26-27 years when leaving the School),[1] of the probationers. Though it is too early, yet, to pass a final judgment on such a young institution, it can be safely asserted that it has fulfilled the tasks assigned to it, and that it will continue to do so in the future.

* * *

Let us now try to conclude this comparative study. I do not, for a moment, suggest or believe that the English and the French systems of recruitment and training of higher civil servants, by reciprocal borrowing from each other, are about to merge into one. Tradition, environment, forms of thought are too different in our two countries. Still, I venture to think that the French system, at the level of recruitment, will have to originate new techniques in order to give more importance to the evaluation of the candidates as a whole and to qualities other than those which are purely intellectual. On the other hand, I consider it probable that the British will feel obliged to strike a new balance between 'a liberal education' and the ever-growing importance of the social sciences in the welfare state and its administration. I believe, also, that, in one form or another, a professional training school or centre will be set up in Great Britain for the young civil servants. This is a world-wide tendency today, in the development of which France has played a pioneer rôle. Other nations have since followed its example, including India and Pakistan. United Nations Institutes of Public Administration have been established in Brazil, Turkey, Costa Rica, Egypt. It's a long way to . . . London, perhaps, but even where the Civil Service is concerned, the days of insularity may soon belong to the past.

[1] The upper age limits, for the entrance examination, are twenty-six for the students and thirty for civil servants. But periods of service in the Armed Forces are to be deducted and, also, one year is deducted per child, without any limitation, for candidates who have a family. Besides, all ex-students who have not yet done their military service, must do it before entering the school—which means that they enter it only two years later. Personally, I consider it advisable that these age limits be lowered, and a maximum period of deduction of, say, three or four years, be laid down.

INDEX

INDEX

INDEX

Democracy in administration, 4-15, 53-4, 168-9
in France, 162-3, 169
parliamentary questions and, 20
Departmental Classes, 46, 58
Departments, and establishments, 119-20, 127-36
origins of, 48
size of, 98-9
and training, 41-2, 58, 138, 179-80
Direction de la Fonction Publique, 171
Discipline, 1, 120, 127, 164, 167-8
Dreyfus Affair, 164

École Libre des Sciences Politiques, 172, 174
École Nationale d'Administration, 58, 171, 173, 175-8, 180-4
Economic affairs, 33, 49, 52-3, 55, 121-2
Education, Ministry of, 15, 43, 48, 51
Establishments, 103, 119-21, 124-38, 171
Examinations, for entry to Civil Service, 26, 27, 35-7, 44, 170-1, 184
for Administrative Class, 38-41 55-8, 155-6, 158, 160, 175-9
for Commonwealth Relations Service, 69
for Departmental Classes, 46, 58
for Executive and Clerical Classes, 37, 58
for Foreign Service, 64-5
in France, 167, 170-8, 182
for Professional and Scientific Staffs, 44-6
Exchequer, Chancellor of; *see* Chancellor of Exchequer

Executive Class, location of, 43
numbers in, 99
promotion from, 153, 157
recruitment to, 37, 46, 58

Farrer, Sir Thomas: Treasury control, 115-16
Finance, departmental responsibility for, 113
Parliamentary control of, 109-11, 117
Treasury control of, 109-19
Fisher, Sir Warren: Administrative Class, 104-6, 116
departmental control of finance, 113
Treasury control, 104-6, 107-8, 116
Flynn, Sir Albert, 156
Foreign Office, 48, 51-2, 61-3, 171
and formulation of foreign policy, 61, 71, 74-80
organisation of, 75, 78-80
Foreign Service, 61, 63, 79-80, 106
Bevin and, 18, 73
compulsory retirement from, 66-7, 106
criticism of, by Select Committee on Estimates, 73-4
duties of, 68-9, 71-2, 76-7
entertainment and living standards in, 72-4, 80
numbers, 61, 99
promotion in, 66-8
recruitment to, 63-6, 80
social background of, 14, 61, 65
Francs Case, 7
French Civil Service, 10-11, 161-6, 168-9
discipline of, 167-8
promotion in, 167

187

INDEX